ANIMAL SUPERSTARS
biggest, strongest, fastest, smartest

ANIMAL SUPERSTARS
biggest, strongest, fastest, smartest

by Russell Freedman

Prentice-Hall, Inc.
Englewood Cliffs, New Jersey

Frontispiece photo (opposite title page): *Marineland of Florida*

Design by Ronnie Ann Herman

Prentice-Hall International, Inc., London
Prentice-Hall of Australia, Pty. Ltd., North Sydney
Prentice-Hall of Canada, Ltd., Toronto
Prentice-Hall of India Private Ltd., New Delhi
Prentice-Hall of Japan, Inc., Tokyo
Prentice-Hall of Southeast Asia Pte. Ltd., Singapore
Whitehall Books Limited, Wellington, New Zealand

10 9 8 7 6 5 4 3 2

Library of Congress Cataloging in Publication Data

Freedman, Russell.
  Animal superstars.

  Includes index.
  Summary: Spotlights animals that possess note-
worthy abilities or physical attributes.
    1. Animals—Miscellanea—Juvenile literature.
[1. Animals—Miscellanea]   I. Title.
QL49.F853   591   81-8503
ISBN 0-13-037648-5   AACR2

contents

author's note

This is a book of facts and figures about exceptional animals. They are exceptional because they jump higher, dive deeper, travel farther, live longer, or have more babies than other animals; or because they are bigger, faster, stronger, hungrier, or smarter.

How do we know which animals are the biggest, the fastest, the strongest, the smartest? The fact is, we don't always know. It is easy enough to measure the size and weight of an animal in captivity. However, eyewitness accounts of giant animals in the wild are not always based on actual measurements, so those accounts may differ. And when it comes to abilities like speed, strength, and intelligence, exact measurements may not be possible.

So along with established facts and figures, you'll find estimates, guesses, and disagreements as you read this book. Experts don't agree on the top speeds of the fastest animals. They can only guess at the strength of many wild animals. And they don't know how smart the smartest animals really are.

Since experts disagree among themselves, books disagree too. The figures given in this book have been selected from many different sources. They are the author's choice as the most authoritative and up-to-date figures currently available.

Unusual traits and outstanding abilities are always interesting. And yet, if we look closely enough, we find that every living creature possesses unique and special qualities. The most common and ordinary animals are superstars in their own right, because they know how to survive.

metric conversion table

Use these formulas to convert measurements given in this book to their metric equivalents.

1 inch = 2.54 centimeters
To find length in centimeters, multiply number of inches by 2.5.

1 foot = 0.3048 meters (1 meter = 100 centimeters)
To find length in meters, multiply number of feet by 0.3.

1 mile = 1.609 kilometers (1 kilometer = 1,000 meters)
To find length in kilometers, multiply number of miles by 1.6.

1 ounce = 28.350 grams
To find weight in grams, multiply number of ounces by 28.3.

1 pound = 0.453 kilograms (1 kilogram = 1,000 grams)
To find weight in kilograms, multiply number of pounds by 0.45.

1 ton = 0.907 metric ton (1 metric ton = 1,000 kilograms)
To find weight in metric tons, multiply number of tons by 0.9.

1 gallon = 3.785 liters
To find volume in liters, multiply number of gallons by 3.8.

For Rose
a champ in any league

the fastest animals

The giant land tortoise is not one of the world's fastest animals. In the Seychelles Islands, a tortoise in a hurry was clocked at the top speed of 0.23 miles an hour. At that rate, it could "run" the mile in about 4 hours and 20 minutes.

A snail's pace is even slower. Crawling as fast as it possibly could, a common garden snail would take 32 hours to go a mile.

Snakes slither along at about one-half mile an hour, but they can move faster when they are frightened. The fastest snakes in North America are racers and whipsnakes. A coachwhip has been timed at 3.6 miles an hour. That's brisk walking speed for a person.

In an open field, you could easily outdistance any North American snake. But on rough ground or in thick underbrush, a racer or whipsnake can move faster than a person, and it can change direction abruptly without slowing down.

The world's fastest snake is the deadly black mamba of East Africa. It grows to a length of 14 feet, and when it strikes, it can reach a person's head. Black mambas have been timed at 7 miles an hour. In short bursts of speed they may reach 15 miles an hour. You probably can't run that fast.

Could you outrun an elephant? Not unless you're an Olympic champion—and an elephant can't even run. An elephant ambles—it lifts both legs on its left side at the same time and swings them forward, then it lifts both legs on its right side. That's why it rolls from side to side like a ship as it ambles along.

An elephant's stout legs are designed to carry its great weight. They aren't built for running or galloping. Even so, an elephant can move fast when it wants to. Charging elephants have been timed at a top speed of 24 miles an hour.

The fastest speed ever reached by a woman runner in Olympic competition is 24 miles an hour—tying the elephant. The record speed for a man in the Olympics is 27 miles an hour.

An ostrich can leave an Olympic runner far behind. Ostriches can't fly, but they can skim across the African plains at 35 miles an hour. And they can keep up that pace for at least 30 minutes. In short bursts of speed, the ostrich has been timed at 43.5 miles an hour—making it faster than a racehorse. It's the fastest bird on two legs.

For many creatures, speed is a matter of life or death. Rabbits are among the swiftest small animals. A frightened jack rabbit explodes suddenly into full flight. As it bounds away, its long hind legs and big feet strike the ground together. Dodging and zigzagging, it can reach a top speed of about 45 miles an hour.

Large grazing animals also depend on sudden bursts of speed to escape their enemies. At full speed, many deer and antelope can do up to 50 miles an hour. The swiftest grazing animal is probably the pronghorn antelope, which roams the western plains of North America. A pronghorn pursued by an enemy can exceed 60 miles an hour.

12

TOP RUNNING SPEEDS

Animal	Maximum Recorded Speed (mph)
Garden Snail	0.03
Giant Tortoise	0.23
Black Mamba Snake	7+
House Mouse	8
Sheep	11
Racerunner Lizard	18
Elephant	24
Human	27
Black Rhinoceros	28
Cat	30
Grizzly Bear	30
Lion	36
Giraffe	37
Wolf	40
Greyhound	42
Racehorse	43.3
Ostrich	43.5
Jack Rabbit	45
White-tailed Deer	50
Thomson's Gazelle	50
Pronghorn Antelope	61
Cheetah	71

The fastest land animal of all is a hunter—the sleek cheetah. Experts agree that over a short course, a cheetah can outrun any other animal. But they don't agree on its top speed. According to one expert, French naturalist François Bourlière, a cheetah clocked from a speeding automobile covered 700 yards in 20 seconds, averaging just over 71 miles an hour.

The cheetah's powers of acceleration are even more impressive than its bursts of speed. It can go from a standing start to 45 miles an hour in 2 seconds—a performance that can't be matched by the fastest racing car.

The secret of the cheetah's speed lies in its supple spine. As it runs, its spine bends like a spring. This allows the cheetah to bring its hind legs well forward on each leap and gives it a long stride. At the start of the next leap, its spine straightens out, giving added thrust to its powerful hind legs.

This springlike bounding has one drawback: it takes great

Cheetah in action: as fast as 70 miles per hour. *American Museum of Natural History*

energy. A cheetah can maintain its top speed for only a few hundred yards before tiring and slowing down. It is a champion sprinter, not a long-distance runner.

When a cheetah spots a herd of gazelles, it moves slowly toward them against the wind. It "freezes" instantly if any of the animals seem to be looking its way. As soon as it is close enough, it bounds forward in a short burst of speed. It must capture its prey during that first fast sprint. Antelopes and gazelles have greater endurance than a cheetah, and with enough warning they can usually escape.

An Olympic runner can reach 27 miles an hour, but the top speed for an Olympic swimmer is only 5 miles an hour. The human body is not streamlined to cut easily through the water. We're just not built for fast swimming.

A sea otter can swim twice as fast as a person, a walrus three times as fast. Whales and dolphins can shoot through the water at 25 miles an hour or more.

Among birds, penguins are the best swimmers. They can't fly, but they can zip through the water faster than many birds

TOP SWIMMING SPEEDS

Animal	Maximum Recorded Speed (mph)
Shrimp	2
Human	5
Beaver	6
Eel	8
Sea Otter	10
Striped Bass	12
Walrus	15
Mackerel	20
Leatherback Turtle	22
Gentoo Penguin	22+
Blue Whale	23
Sea Lion	25
Barracuda	27
Dolphin	29
Flying Fish	35
Blue Shark	40
Tuna	43
Marlin	50
Swordfish	58
Sailfish	68

fly through the air. They use their wings as flippers (flapping them under the water) and their feet as rudders. In the Antarctic, penguins have been timed swimming under water at 22.5 miles an hour. They probably reach a top speed of 30 miles an hour.

Marlins and tuna are among the fastest fish. They can reach speeds of 40 to 50 miles an hour—faster than an ocean liner. A swordfish can approach 60 miles an hour—fast enough to drive its sharp bill deep into the wooden hull of a boat.

The fastest swimmer in the sea is the sailfish. A sailfish off the coast of Florida was clocked at a top speed of 68 miles an hour. That's almost twice the speed of the world's fastest nuclear submarines.

An insect called the deer botfly was once considered the speed champion of the world. Dr. Charles Townsend studied the deer botfly in 1926. His field observations indicated that the insect could fly at the rate of 440 yards per second, or 820 miles an hour!

Dr. Townsend published his findings in a respected scientific journal: "On 12,000-foot summits in New Mexico, I have seen pass me at an incredible velocity what were certainly the males of [the deer botfly]. I could barely distinguish that something had passed—only a brownish blur in the air about the right size for these flies.

"The time was checked repeatedly with the shutter of a camera," Dr. Townsend wrote. "The data are practically accurate and as close as ever will be possible to measure."

Years later, studies proved that no insect can possibly fly that fast. At such a speed, air friction would make it burn up.

The famous case of the deer botfly shows how difficult it is to measure the flying speed of any creature. Today we have

TOP FLYING SPEEDS

Animal	Maximum Recorded Speed (mph)
Housefly	5
Monarch Butterfly	10+
Honeybee	14
Blue Jay	20
Pelican	28
Sparrow	35
Dragonfly	36+
Herring Gull	38
Great Horned Owl	40
Barn Swallow	46
Starling	50
Wild Turkey	58
Canada Goose	60
Mallard Duck	65
Canvasback Duck	70
Wandering Albatross	77
Golden Eagle	80
Racing Pigeon	90
Spine-tailed Swift	106+
Peregrine Falcon	240 (power dive)

better methods of estimating flying speed than Dr. Townsend had, but it's still a tricky business. Different methods give different results.

Because insects are small, they often seem faster than they really are. When you watch a housefly buzzing around the room, it seems to be flying at a great speed. Actually, it is traveling at no more than 5 miles an hour.

As a rule, large insects fly faster than small ones. The fastest insects in the air are dragonflies. It is possible that some

Peregrine falcon: the world's fastest living creature? *G. Ronald Austing/Photo Researchers*

dragonflies can fly up to 40 or 50 miles an hour for short distances. However, the top speed actually measured for a dragonfly is 36 miles an hour. That's a far cry from Dr. Townsend's measurement, but it's faster than many birds can fly.

Scientists have used many different methods to measure the flying speeds of birds. Birds have been clocked from the ground, followed in airplanes, tracked by radar, and tested in special wind tunnels. As with insects, the results do not always agree. When bird experts get together, nothing starts an argument more quickly than the flying speeds of birds.

Most small birds fly at air speeds ranging from 20 to 30 miles an hour, although swallows and starlings are faster. Hawks cruise along at 40 miles an hour. Ducks and geese commonly reach 60 miles an hour or more. Golden eagles have been timed at 80 miles an hour. Racing pigeons have been clocked in flight tests at a top speed of 90 miles an hour.

The fastest birds are falcons and swifts. They have swept-back pointed wings, like those of a jet plane. Swifts, found throughout the world, spend all their active hours in the air. They feed, drink, bathe, mate, and gather nesting materials on the wing. Their usual flight speed is between 60 and 70 miles an hour, but they can easily exceed 100 miles an hour. In Russia, a spine-tailed swift was reliably clocked at 106 miles an hour.

Some swifts may be able to fly much faster than that. In India during the 1930s, a British scientist named E. C. Stuart-Baker tried to measure the speed of spine-tailed swifts that flew directly over his house every day. The birds traveled in a straight line to a ridge of hills 2 miles away, where they dropped out of sight. Stuart-Baker and several companions watched the swifts with binoculars and timed them with stopwatches. According to their calculations, the fastest swifts covered the 2-mile course in 41.8 and 32.8 seconds, or at the rate of 172 and 218 miles an hour, respectively.

Today, many experts question the accuracy of Stuart-Baker's figures. But they agree that swifts are probably the fastest birds in level flight.

The speed of falcons is also a matter of debate. In level flight, these powerful bullet-headed birds can top 100 miles an hour. When they are diving after prey, they may travel more than twice that fast.

As a falcon dives, it folds its wings against its body, making it more missile-shaped than bird-shaped. The speed of the falcon's power dive has been estimated at anywhere from 80 to 200 miles an hour or more.

How much more? In 1970, two scientists, V. A. Tucker and G. C. Parrott, studied a peregrine falcon, or duck hawk, that had been trained to fly in a wind tunnel. They reported their results in the *Journal of Experimental Biology.* Tucker and Parrott estimated that the maximum speed of a falcon during its power dive is about 100 meters per second—or about 240 miles an hour. That would make the falcon far and away the world's fastest living creature.

champion jumpers
and divers

The human body is not built for great speed, but as jumpers we do surprisingly well. Olympic champions have jumped as high as 7 feet 8 inches and as far as 29 feet 2½ inches. Not many animals can do better than that.

Africa's best jumper is an antelope, the impala. At any hint of danger, herds of impala take off and race for safety. The animals bound away, stretching their bodies in a series of spectacular twisting leaps. An impala can leap 10 feet into the air. It can cover a distance of 35 feet or more in a single leap.

A champion jumping horse, spurred on by a rider, can't do as well as a wild impala. The official record for horses in the high jump is 8 feet 1¼ inches; the record for the long jump is 27 feet 2¾ inches. Unofficially, horses have been credited with jumps as high as 9½ feet and as long as 37 feet.

The most powerful jumper in North America is the puma, also known as the cougar, or mountain lion. Pumas hunt at night in remote wilderness areas. They wait in ambush, then leap upon their prey. The highest leap recorded for a puma is 12 feet; the longest is 39 feet.

The longest jumps of all are made by Australia's kangaroos. Normally, a kangaroo walks on all fours. When it speeds up, it starts hopping on its hind legs. It holds its body forward, keeps its short front legs tucked up, and uses its outstretched tail as a balance.

As a kangaroo bounds along, both hind legs hit the ground at the same time. At a slow pace, it covers 4 to 6 feet with each hop. When it is being chased, it can leap 10 feet into the air and cover 30 feet or more in a single bound. The longest jump ever recorded for a kangaroo is 42 feet—about 8 times the length of its body. An Olympic jumper, by comparison, jumps about 5 times the length of his body.

Kangaroos jump farther than any other animal, but they aren't the best jumpers for their size. A jack rabbit is much smaller than a kangaroo, yet it can leap over a 6-foot fence and jump 15 or 20 feet in a single bound. One jack rabbit, running for its life, made a leap of 22 feet 4 inches, by actual measurement—11 times the length of its body.

CHAMPION BROAD JUMPERS

Animal	Longest Recorded Jump
Common Flea	13 inches
Field Cricket	24 inches
Grasshopper	30 inches
Kangaroo Rat	8 feet
Jerboa	10 feet
Jumping Mouse	12 feet
Frog	17 feet 6¾ inches
Jumping Hare	20 feet
Jack Rabbit	22 feet 4 inches
Human	29 feet 2½ inches
Impala	35+ feet
Horse	37 feet
Puma	39 feet
Kangaroo	42 feet

Jerboas are small rodents from Asia and Africa that hop on their hind legs like miniature kangaroos. A jerboa is only about 6 inches long, but it can jump 10 feet in a single bound—20 times the length of its body.

The best jumper for its size among the mammals is the beautiful little jumping mouse. Jumping mice are common throughout North America, but they are rarely noticed because they are so small. They are sometimes seen on moonlit nights, disappearing into the darkness with mighty leaps.

A jumping mouse weighs less than an ounce. It is between 3 and 4 inches long, not counting its tail. When it is startled, it makes several zigzag jumps ranging from 4 to 7 feet in length. If a jumping mouse is really frightened, it can leap 10 or even 12 feet at a single bound—more than 30 times the length of its body. If a man had the jumping power of a jumping mouse, he could leap across a football field in two easy bounds.

Insects are noted for their jumping ability; yet a jumping mouse can do better for its size than some well-known jumping insects. A grasshopper's 30-inch jump is equal to 20 times the length of its body.

Two kangaroos sail through the air near an Australian lake. *Australian Information Service*

The world's champion jumper, however, does happen to be an insect—the common flea. A flea can't fly because it has no wings, but it makes up for that with its high and wide leaps. Its legs, about $\frac{1}{20}$ inch long, are packed with the greatest muscle power of any legs in the animal world.

A flea can jump as high as 7¾ inches and as far as 13 inches. That doesn't seem like much compared to the 42-foot jump of a kangaroo or even the 30-inch jump of a grasshopper. But for a tiny flea it is an amazing performance. Some fleas can jump 200 times the length of their bodies. An equivalent leap for a 6-foot man would carry him the length of 5 city blocks.

The booby prize for jumping goes to the elephant. An elephant can't jump at all, not even an inch.

A gannet is a sea bird that dives for its dinner. It plunges from the sky and hits the water with such force that fish below the surface are stunned. The gannet has a sharply pointed beak, but it doesn't spear fish. Instead, it swirls beneath them and grabs them on the way up. Gannets have been known to dive to a depth of 90 feet.

A loon dives abruptly while swimming on the surface. It can hold its breath for about 5 minutes and swim hundreds of yards under water while chasing a fish. One loon reached a depth of 240 feet, where it was caught in a fisherman's net.

Penguins, the best swimmers among birds, are also the deepest divers. They dive to hunt for squid, shrimp, and cuttlefish. An emperor penguin usually makes a quick dive that lasts only a minute or two, but if necessary, it can stay submerged for over 18 minutes. Emperor penguins equipped with depth recorders and observed from underwater chambers have reached depths of 885 feet below the surface.

25

An emperor penguin begins its dive. It can hold its breath for at least 18 minutes and reach a depth of more than 800 feet. *New York Zoological Society*

CHAMPION DEEP DIVERS

Animal	Deepest Recorded Dive (in feet)
Gannet	90
Grebe	100
Sea Otter	100+
Cormorant	135
Duck	210
Loon	240
Walrus	300
Human Scuba Diver	437
Gray Seal	500+
Sea Lion	600
Emperor Penguin	885
Dolphin	1,000+
Fin Whale	1,150
Weddell Seal	1,970
Sperm Whale	3,720

Mammals that live at sea also dive for their food. Sea otters plunge 100 feet or more to feed on abalone, sea urchins, and crabs. Walruses explore the bottom at depths of 300 feet, where they use their long tusks to dredge up shellfish. Sea lions search for fish at 600 feet. Fin whales plunge to depths of 1,000 feet. And a Weddell seal is on record as diving 1,970 feet in McMurdo Sound, Antarctica.

The sperm whale is the champion underwater diver among air-breathing animals. It can hold its breath for nearly 2 hours, probably longer, as it hunts for giant squid on the ocean floor. Sperm whales have reached a recorded depth of 3,720 feet, and there is evidence that they go much deeper than that.

Few humans can hold their breath safely for more than 2 minutes. A dog can swim under water for 4 or 5 minutes at most before coming up for air. Yet some seals and whales can

CHAMPION BREATH-HOLDERS

Animal	Longest Recorded Stay Under Water (in minutes)
Muskrat	12
Southern Elephant Seal	12
Beaver	15
Emperor Penguin	18
Gray Seal	20
Fin Whale	30
Blue Whale	49
Weddell Seal	70
Greenland Right Whale	80
Sperm Whale	112
Bottlenose Whale	120

stay under water for an hour or longer. How can they hold their breath so long?

Seagoing mammals breathe more efficiently than we do. With each breath, a whale changes about 90 percent of the air in its lungs. Humans change only about 15 to 20 percent. By emptying and refilling its lungs almost completely, the whale sucks in a large supply of fresh oxygen before it dives under water.

As it begins its dive, the whale's heartbeat slows down. This means that it uses its supply of oxygen more slowly, and it can stay submerged for a long time. The record for breath-holding goes to the bottlenose whale, which can stay under for at least 2 hours without coming up for air.

long-distance travelers

A monarch butterfly weighs little more than half a gram (about $\frac{1}{50}$ ounce). It flutters along at 10 miles an hour, reaches 30 miles an hour in short bursts, and flies 600 miles on a single "tankful" of nectar.

Every fall, millions of these black-and-orange butterflies travel south from Canada and northern areas of the United States. Scientists trace their migration routes by pasting identification tags on their wings. One monarch tagged near Lake Ontario in Canada was recaptured 4 months later near the town of Catorce, Mexico—1,870 miles away. Other monarchs are believed to travel at least 2,400 miles one way between Canada and Mexico.

The butterflies spend the winter along the Gulf of Mexico and the coast of California. In spring they head north again, laying their eggs on milkweed plants along the way. They fly as far north into Canada as milkweed grows.

Monarchs live less than a year. Most of the butterflies die on their way north, but a few survive long enough to complete a round trip back to Canada. During their brief lifetimes, these frail insects may travel 4,000 miles or more.

Long migratory journeys are made by about 250 different kinds of butterflies; by other insects such as moths, dragonflies, and locusts; and by a wide variety of fishes, reptiles, birds, and mammals. Billions of creatures migrate every year. Flying, swimming, walking, or crawling, they follow paths laid down by their ancestors as they travel between their summer and winter homes.

Caribou are the world's champion walkers. Some caribou spend the winter in Canadian forests. In spring they trudge north through melting snows to graze in the arctic tundra, far beyond the timberline. They spend the summer near the shores of the Arctic Ocean and then head back to the forests, traveling together in great herds. Their yearly journey may involve more than 1,000 miles of walking.

Chinook salmon are famous for their spectacular one-way journey up the Yukon River. They spend most of their lives far out at sea in the North Pacific. When the time comes to migrate, they head for the coast of Alaska and enter the mouth of the Yukon.

Fighting against rapids, leaping 8 or 10 feet up waterfalls, the salmon battle their way up the Yukon. As they move upstream, they begin to branch off into smaller and smaller streams, heading for the place where they were born. Each salmon is guided by its keen sense of smell. It chooses which stream to enter by the water's chemical odor. With unerring accuracy, it is led by its nose all the way back to its birthplace. From the time a chinook salmon starts this once-in-a-lifetime journey home, it may travel more than 1,000 miles across the open sea and another 2,000 miles up the Yukon.

The longest journeys at sea are made by an air-breathing mammal, the California gray whale. Gray whales spend the

A herd of caribou migrate toward their summer feeding grounds.
Charlie Ott/Photo Researchers

winter in warm lagoons along the coast of Mexico. As spring approaches, they set out for their summer feeding grounds in the Arctic Ocean. The whales cruise along at 4 knots, swimming 70 or 80 miles every 24 hours. They do not pause to eat on the journey north, and they sleep little, if at all. Their trip covers between 4,000 and 6,000 miles and takes 3 months of steady swimming.

During the summer, the whales gorge themselves on plankton in icy arctic waters. Then they spend 3 months swimming back to their winter homes in sheltered Mexican lagoons.

Birds are the greatest long-distance travelers of all. In North America alone, an estimated 20 billion birds migrate every year. Some, like robins and crows, fly just a few hundred miles between their summer and winter homes. Others travel thousands of miles across the equator. By migrating, they enjoy two summers each year and never know the chill of winter.

North American swallows travel up to 9,000 miles one way, from their breeding grounds in Alaska to their winter homes in Patagonia, at the southern tip of South America. European swallows travel almost as far, flying about 8,000 miles from Scandinavia to South Africa.

Golden plovers nest in the arctic tundra, where they find plenty of food and space during the brief arctic summer. Toward the end of summer, the adult plovers leave their growing young behind. They fly east across Canada to Nova Scotia and Newfoundland. Then they turn south and fly nonstop over the Atlantic to Argentina—a one-way trip of 8,000 to 10,000 miles.

YEARLY MIGRATIONS

Animal	Migration Route	Distance One Way (in miles)
Caribou	Arctic tundra to Canadian forests	400–500
Green Sea Turtle	Coast of Brazil to Ascension Island	1,400
Red Bat	Labrador to Bermuda	1,400
Monarch Butterfly	Canada to Gulf of Mexico	1,500–2,000
Chinook Salmon	North Pacific to Alaska and up the Yukon	3,000
Alaskan Fur Seal	Pribilof Islands to California coast	3,000
California Gray Whale	Arctic Ocean to Mexican coast	4,000–6,000
Willow Warbler	Siberia to southern Africa	6,000
Bobolink	Canada to Argentina	7,000
White Stork	Northern Europe to South Africa	8,000
European Barn Swallow	Scandinavia to South Africa	8,000
American Barn Swallow	Alaska to Patagonia	9,000
White-rumped Sandpiper	Canadian Arctic to Patagonia	9,000
American Golden Plover	Canadian Arctic to Argentina	8,000–10,000
Arctic Tern	Arctic Circle to Antarctica	10,000–12,000

A short time later, the young plovers begin their first migration by themselves, without the help of experienced adults. They even take a different route, staying over land all the way. They fly south over Canada, the United States, Mexico, and Central America. Then they head directly for Argentina. Guided only by their inborn sense of direction, they join their parents in the Argentine grasslands.

The champion long-distance migrant is the streamer-tailed arctic tern, a cousin of the common sea gull. These birds breed during the summer along the northernmost ice-free shores of the Arctic Ocean. Some arctic terns build their nests within a few degrees of the North Pole.

As summer ends, the birds set off on the longest journey made by any animal. They fly from the Arctic Circle to the seas of Antarctica, a distance of 10,000 to 12,000 miles. Arctic terns see more hours of daylight every year than any other living creature.

Scientists have mapped the migration routes of many different animals. We know where these animals go as they travel back and forth in tune with the seasons. But how do they find their way? How do they return year after year to the same fields, forests, beaches, and islands?

White storks fly from their winter quarters in South Africa to their summer nesting sites in northern Europe, a one-way trip of about 8,000 miles. Each year the storks return to the same towns and villages in Holland and Germany where they themselves were born. They even return to the same rooftop nests they used the year before.

Experiments have shown that birds and many other migrating animals steer by the sun or the stars. They are able to

Arctic tern: from the Arctic to the Antarctic and back. *Karl H. Maslowski/Photo Researchers*

set their course by watching the sun or stars move across the sky. Some animals, such as salmon, are guided by their sense of smell during migrations. Migrating animals may also be sensitive to the earth's magnetic pull, to the earth's rotation, to the ultraviolet light coming from the sun, and even to low-frequency sounds coming from the earth. Any or all of these may be used as navigational aids. Animals find their way across vast distances by using a combination of senses we do not fully understand.

This mysterious sense of direction seems to be shared even by animals that usually stay close to home. An alligator rarely strays more than a few hundred yards from its den. Yet in an experiment, an alligator kidnapped from its Florida cypress swamp, sealed in a dark box, and released in strange territory 20 miles from home eventually showed up at its home den.

Similar experiments indicate that animals as different as mice, ants, pigs, and bats have this same inexplicable homing ability. One of the most impressive homing feats on record belongs to a small bird, a Manx shearwater. The bird was taken from its nest on the island of Skokholm off the coast of Wales. It was placed in a box, put aboard a plane, and flown 3,050 miles to Logan Airport in Boston. Then it was set free. The shearwater set out across the unknown Atlantic. It arrived at its nest on Skokholm Island 12½ days later.

big, bigger, and biggest

Science fiction movies sometimes show giant insects threatening to take over the earth. That makes a good story—but it's fiction, not science. Insects have never been much bigger than they are today, and they never will be.

Insects are small because of the way their bodies are built. An insect has no bones inside its body. Instead, it has a tough outer shell called an *exoskeleton*, which holds its body together and serves as a protective coat of armor.

This body design works well for a small creature, but it wouldn't work for a big one. As insects get bigger, their outer shells become bulkier and heavier. An insect the size of a dog or a horse wouldn't be able to haul its bulky exoskeleton around.

The smallest insects are barely big enough to see. One of the smallest is a North American beetle about $\frac{1}{100}$ inch long. It can easily creep through the eye of a needle. Tiny wasps called fairy flies are as small or smaller. A fairy fly is slightly larger than the period at the end of this sentence.

Some moths and butterflies are a thousand times bigger than a fairy fly. The Atlas moth of India measures 12 inches from wingtip to wingtip—a wingspread nearly as great as that of an oriole.

The world's bulkiest insect is the Goliath beetle of Africa, which sounds like an approaching airplane as it drones over the countryside at dusk. Some of these beetles are 5 to 6 inches long and weigh nearly ¼ pound, making them longer and heavier than some rats. The Goliath beetle likes to eat bananas, which it peels with its snout.

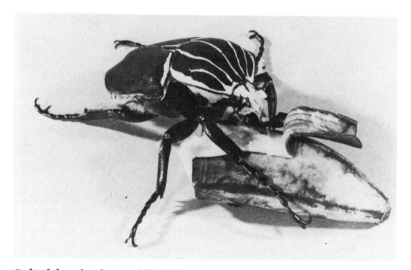

Goliath beetle: the world's bulkiest insect. *American Museum of Natural History*

Each group of animals has its giants. The biggest lizard—the Komodo monitor or dragon lizard of the East Indies—is the size of a small horse. A dragon lizard may be 10 feet long and weigh up to 365 pounds. It has a flicking tongue like a snake; it hisses and lashes its tail and fights with its teeth and claws. Dragon lizards are big enough to run down wild pigs and swallow them whole.

The biggest crocodile is a dangerous man-eater—the saltwater crocodile of Southeast Asia. An average saltwater crocodile is about 12 feet long, but some individuals reach lengths of 20 feet or more. The biggest saltwater crocodile ever found was killed in the Philippines in 1823. It was 27 feet long and weighed more than 2 tons.

Pythons and anacondas are the biggest snakes. They are constrictors that coil about their prey and squeeze until it suffocates. Indian pythons have been known to swallow deer with 12-inch horns. And there is an authenticated report from Southeast Asia of a reticulated python eating a bear that probably weighed 200 pounds.

The longest snake ever accurately measured by a scientist was a 33-foot reticulated python killed in the jungles of Indonesia. However, some South American anacondas may grow longer than any python. Since anacondas live in the swamps and rivers of remote jungles, they are rarely seen. There are reliable reports of an anaconda shot by an engineering party in Colombia. Measured with a steel tape, it was 37½ feet long—longer than six tall men lying head to foot. It probably weighed about 1,000 pounds.

The wandering albatross has the longest wings of any creature flying today. It may measure nearly 12 feet from wingtip to wingtip—almost as long as two beds placed end to end. And yet an albatross weighs only about 20 pounds. Its light body and long tapering wings make it the best long-distance glider of any bird. Swept along by sea winds, an albatross can glide for hours without flapping its wings.

The biggest bird living today is the flightless ostrich, which is much too heavy to get off the ground. A large ostrich may weigh 345 pounds, as much as a Shetland pony. It may stand

An ostrich egg compared to a hummingbird egg. *American Museum of Natural History*

9 feet tall—too tall to walk through a door. Its small head overlooks most other animals on the African plains.

As you might expect, the ostrich lays the biggest eggs of any bird. A creamy white ostrich egg is from 6 to 8 inches long—longer than your hand. If you scrambled an ostrich egg, it would serve 12 people. If you hardboiled it, you'd have to wait 40 minutes before it was done.

Gorillas are the biggest apes. A full-grown gorilla may be 6 feet tall. He has an armspread of 8 feet. And he weighs about 450 muscular pounds. The tallest gorilla ever measured stood 6 feet 2 inches tall. The heaviest gorilla ever weighed tipped the scales at 670 pounds.

The biggest flesh-eating mammal on earth is Alaska's Kodiak bear, a member of the grizzly bear family. A large male measures 9 feet from his nose to his tail. When he rears up on his hind legs, he may be 12 feet tall. Bears do not kill their prey with a deathly hug, as some people believe, but with a powerful swat of the paw.

The tallest animal on earth is the giraffe. Its neck alone may be 7 or 8 feet long. A giraffe likes to eat the tender leaves and twigs at the top of acacia trees, which it reaches with the help of its 17-inch-long tongue.

A few giraffes are more than 19 feet tall—tall enough to look into a second-story window. Because of its long neck, a giraffe needs a big heart to pump blood all the way up to its head. Its heart is 2 feet long and weighs 25 pounds. A human heart is about 5 inches long and weighs about 10 ounces. A giraffe's blood pressure—two to three times that of a healthy person—is probably the highest blood pressure on earth.

Along with the tallest animal, Africa has the three heaviest land animals: the white rhinoceros, the hippopotamus, and the African bush elephant. A full-grown white rhinoceros weighs up to 3 tons, as much as a big limousine. A hippopotamus may weigh 4 tons. Some African elephants weigh 6 tons or more—twice as much as a rhino and a third more than a hippo. (Remember, one ton is 2,000 pounds.)

The elephants we see in zoos and circuses are usually female Indian elephants. As a rule, Indian elephants are smaller than African elephants, and females of both species are smaller than males. So unless you've been to an African game preserve, you've probably never seen a really big elephant. A 6-ton African bull elephant stands about 11 feet high at the shoulder—higher than the baskets in a regulation basketball court.

African elephants of both sexes have tusks, and the males usually have the longest ones. The biggest pair of tusks ever found are on exhibit at the Bronx Zoo in New York—one tusk is 11 feet long, the other 11 feet 5½ inches. Together they weigh 293 pounds.

Although 6 tons is usually the top weight for an African elephant, a few individuals grow heavier than that. The famous elephant Jumbo of the Barnum and Bailey Circus weighed about 13,000 pounds. The heaviest elephant ever accurately weighed by a scientist was a 14,641-pound male bush elephant shot in Africa. However, another bush elephant, shot in Angola in 1974, was reported to be almost twice that heavy. This elephant measured 13 feet 8 inches tall at the shoulder. Its estimated weight was 26,000 pounds— about 13 tons. That's as heavy as an army tank.

While elephants are the biggest land animals, they are midgets compared to some of the giant animals that live in the sea. A land animal's size is limited by the ability of its legs to carry the weight of its body. Any animal supported by four legs can't be much bigger than the biggest elephants. If it were, it wouldn't be able to hold itself up and walk around.

Millions of years ago, during the Age of Reptiles, some dinosaurs were bigger and heavier than any elephant. However, they probably found it difficult to move around. They had to spend much of their time wallowing about in swamps, where the water buoyed them up and helped take the burden off their bones.

In water, an animal does not have to support the weight of its body. When an animal swims, in fact, it is practically weightless. That's why the world's biggest animals are found at sea.

Giraffe: tall enough to eat tender leaves from the tops of trees.
American Museum of Natural History

BIGGEST IN THEIR CLASS

Animal	Maximum Recorded Size	Maximum Recorded Weight
Atlas Moth	12-inch wingspread	0.15 oz.
Goliath Beetle	5 to 6 inches long	3.5 oz.
Komodo Monitor Lizard	10 ft. 2 in. long	365 lbs.
Leatherback Turtle	8 ft. 4 in. long	1,908 lbs.
Saltwater Crocodile	27 ft. long	4,400 lbs. (estimate)
Anaconda	37½ ft. long	1,000 lbs. (estimate)
Wandering Albatross	11 ft. 10 in. wingspread	20 lbs.
Ostrich	9 ft. tall	345 lbs.
Giant Squid	55 ft. long	4,480 lbs. (estimate)
Giant Jellyfish	200 ft. long	———
Beluga Sturgeon	26 ft. 3 in. long	3,250 lbs.
Ocean Sunfish	14 ft. long	5,017 lbs.
Whale Shark	60 ft. 9 in. long	90,000 lbs. (estimate)
Gorilla	6 ft. 2 in. tall	670 lbs.
Bengal Tiger	11 ft. 1 in. long	857 lbs.
Kodiak Bear	9½ ft. long; 12 ft. tall	1,670 lbs.
Elephant Seal	22½ ft. long	9,000 lbs. (estimate)
Giraffe	19 ft. 3 in. tall	2,200 lbs.
African Elephant	13 ft. 8 in. high	26,000 lbs. (estimate)
Blue Whale	110 ft. 9 in. long	200 tons (estimate)

The torpedo-shaped body of a giant squid may be 20 feet long. Reaching out from the squid's body are sucker-bearing tentacles that may be another 35 feet long, for a total length of 55 feet. If a giant squid were placed at the foul line of a bowling alley, it could almost touch the pins with its tentacles.

44

A giant squid seizes its prey with its tentacles. It pulls the victim into its mouth and bites it to death. Giant squids live in the darkest depths of cold northern oceans. Only a few of these creatures have ever been seen alive. They are known mainly through dead squids washed up on beaches, especially along the coast of Newfoundland.

A giant jellyfish has tentacles much longer than those of any giant squid. These creatures live in icy arctic waters. They may be 8 feet across the body and have as many as 800 tentacles, each one armed with dangerous poison stingers. The tentacles trail down into the water. They are sometimes 200 feet long, making the giant jellyfish the world's longest animal. If a giant jellyfish were placed on the roof of a 20-story building, its tentacles would hang down to the street.

The two biggest fish are sharks—the basking shark and the whale shark. Oddly enough, they are the only sharks that are truly harmless. Most sharks will attack anything that moves. Basking sharks and whale sharks, however, live on the smallest form of animal food in the sea. Their diet consists entirely of plankton—the tiny plants and animals that float near the surface of the sea. Both of these sharks are sluggish, mild-mannered creatures. They often lie on the surface, basking in the sun. They are so harmless, in fact, that swimmers have climbed on their backs without disturbing them.

How big are they? Basking sharks reach a length of 45 feet. Whale sharks can be from 50 to 60 feet long. They weigh more than 40 tons. A whale shark is longer than a big racing yacht, and it weighs twice as much.

The biggest animals at sea are air-breathing mammals, the true whales. A full-grown Greenland right whale is about the same length as a whale shark—50 to 60 feet. A sperm whale may be 70 feet long. And a blue whale may be 100 feet long or more. That makes it the largest animal living today. It is probably the biggest creature that has ever lived on earth.

The longest blue whale ever measured was 110 feet long—longer than a railroad passenger car. The heaviest blue whale ever weighed came to 134 tons. However, blue whales gain and lose enormous amounts of weight according to the season. Their top weight has been estimated at 200 tons. That's at least twice as heavy as *Brachiosaurus*, the heaviest dinosaur that ever lived.

A blue whale has blood vessels big enough for a child to crawl through. Its 6-foot-long heart weighs 1,200 pounds. It takes seven strong men to drag the heart of a blue whale across the deck of a whaling ship. The lungs of a blue whale weigh as much as a ton. Its body may be insulated by 20 tons of blubber.

At birth, a baby blue whale is longer and heavier than all but the biggest land animals. The newborn infant weighs 2 tons and is 25 feet long. It drinks 130 gallons of milk a day. It gains 200 pounds every day and grows more than a foot a week. It can swim from the moment it is born, and it stays close to its mother's side until it grows up.

the strongest animals

If someone boasted, "I'm as strong as a horse," would you believe it? Can manpower be equal to horsepower?

Horses did much of our work before we had machines. They pulled wagons and plows, carriages, coaches, and cannons. An old-fashioned workhorse is much bigger than the riding and racing horses we usually see today. One of the most popular breeds of workhorse, the Belgian, may weigh as much as 3,000 pounds.

A big horse has more muscle power than a small one, so it can pull a heavier load. How does a big horse compare in strength to a big man?

There are many ways of testing strength. One method is to use a dynamometer—an instrument that measures force or power. Both horses and humans have been tested for their pulling ability by means of a dynamometer.

Researchers have found that a horse can pull up to 83 percent of its own dead weight. A man, tested in the same way, can pull up to 86 percent of his dead weight. Since horses are bigger than humans, they can pull heavier loads. But pound for pound, a man is stronger than a horse.

How strong are humans compared to chimpanzees and

gorillas, our closest animal relatives? It's easy enough to measure the strength of a domestic horse, which has been trained to pull and pull hard. It's a lot more difficult to test the strength of a wild animal, even in captivity. Apes and other wild creatures aren't used to pulling loads or lifting weights. They aren't usually tested for strength, and when they are, they don't always cooperate.

Chimpanzees are smaller than humans, but they are much stronger. When a chimpanzee is in the mood, it can easily outlift an Olympic weightlifter. At the Bronx Zoo in New York, a 100-pound chimp once lifted a dead weight of 600 pounds—6 times its own body weight. In the Olympics, a champion weightlifter can lift about 4 times his own weight or slightly more, depending on his weight classification. Of course, that requires long training and great effort. Most of us can't lift anywhere near that much without hurting ourselves.

Jane Goodall is a scientist who has spent years studying wild chimpanzees in Africa. She estimates that the average chimp is about three times stronger than the average human. One chimp raced through the middle of a big supply tent at Goodall's research center, putting on a typical chimpanzee display. As he charged through the tent, he slapped at each of the thick wooden tent poles. The poles snapped in two like matchsticks, one after the other, and the tent collapsed.

A gorilla is about three times bigger than a chimpanzee. A good part of that extra weight is hard muscle, concentrated in the gorilla's massive chest and arms. Gorillas are the strongest apes, but it's hard to tell how strong they really are. They rarely exhibit their strength. They don't prey on other animals, and they try to avoid trouble. Gorillas may look ferocious, but they're actually shy, gentle vegetarians.

Scientist George Schaller, a leading expert on wild gorillas, says that a large male gorilla has "the strength of several men." He notes that a gorilla is strong enough to reach up into a tree and rip down a branch the size of a person's arm.

Full-grown gorillas have no enemies except for human hunters, but young gorillas are sometimes stalked and killed by leopards. Schaller relates a story told by an African native that gives some hint of a gorilla's tremendous power. According to the story, an adult gorilla attacked a leopard that had been threatening young gorillas. The two animals battled hand-to-claw at night, and in the morning the leopard was found dead.

Lions have been respected for their strength since ancient times, when they were first called "the king of beasts." They are certainly the most powerful hunting animals in Africa, and they sometimes chase leopards and cheetahs from their hunting grounds. Lions have been known to kill and eat crocodiles and to crack open tortoise shells. A charging lion can topple over the biggest giraffe. A group of lions can bring down a full-grown hippopotamus.

In Asia, the tiger has long been called "the king of beasts." Tigers are as big as or bigger than lions, and they are just as powerful. Siberian tigers often prey on Himalayan black bears and Siberian brown bears almost their own size. One tiger dragged a full-grown brown bear out of her den, broke her neck, and consumed the carcass during the next week.

The Indians of the American Northwest regarded the grizzly bear as the most powerful creature on earth. Towering 12 feet when it reared up on its hind legs, the grizzly was the biggest and most dangerous animal the Indians knew. An Indian warrior's bear-claw necklace was a proud badge of courage and skill.

A grizzly searching for insects or rodents to eat can flip over boulders like cardboard boxes. When it hunts for big game, it can break the neck of an elk or moose with a powerful blow of its paw. A grizzly has been seen picking up an elk carcass that weighed the better part of a ton and carrying it away.

At one time, grizzlies were recognized as the masters of all wildlife in North America. Today they survive mainly in remote wilderness areas of British Columbia and Alaska. While they can be extremely dangerous, they do not usually attack hunters or campers. But they do raid wilderness camps for food. A grizzly can tear apart a strong wooden commissary box left out by careless campers. It can rip open a can faster than an electric can opener.

As a rule, big animals are more powerful than smaller ones. It isn't surprising, then, that the most powerful land animal is the elephant. Elephants are so big and so powerful, they have no natural enemies except for humans armed with guns. Lions or leopards will sometimes try to attack a small elephant calf that wanders off by itself, but they leave adult elephants strictly alone. No creature on earth can stop an angry African elephant when it makes a full-scale charge.

In Tanzania, an enraged cow elephant charged a Land Rover that had frightened an elephant calf. The big elephant ripped into the side of the Land Rover with her tusks, spinning the car halfway around. Then she rammed the front of the car and started to push. The Land Rover bounced backward like a toy for 35 yards before it crunched against a tree. Its two passengers were lucky to be alive.

Elephants have worked as beasts of burden since ancient times. They played an important role in the Punic Wars of the third century B.C., when the Carthaginian general Hannibal

Indian elephant at work: it can lift a ton of logs with its trunk.
Ylla/Photo Researchers

invaded Italy. Hannibal used elephants to carry heavy baggage and pull military equipment across the steep mountain passes of the Alps.

Indian elephants still do heavy work in the teak forests of Southeast Asia. Asians who train these animals say that a work elephant can lift a ton of logs with its trunk. It can drag a bundle of logs weighing ten tons.

Since great size goes along with great power, the great whales are probably the most powerful animals living today. No one has actually measured a whale's strength, but we can get some idea from attacks made by sperm whales on the ships that hunt them.

Sperm whales are on record as having attacked and sunk four full-sized whaling ships: the *Union* in 1807, the *Essex* in 1820, the *Ann Alexander* in 1851, and the *Kathleen* in 1902. Using their massive heads as battering rams, the whales charged these ships head on. They smashed into the ships' wooden hulls again and again. And when the ships were splintered and foundering, the whales continued to churn the surface, biting at floating debris and crushing the bodies of swimming men.

As recently as 1963, a sperm whale smashed into a fishing launch off the coast of Australia, killing a man.

Blue whales are not as aggressive as sperm whales, and they do not attack ships. But they sometimes display their strength. A 100-ton blue whale carries about 40 tons of muscle, which it uses to propel its gigantic body through the water. When it is frightened, it can surge forward at about 20 miles an hour.

One blue whale was harpooned from a motorized 90-foot catcher boat. As the harpoon hit, the whale took off and tried to escape. It pulled the boat, whose engines were going full-speed astern, for 7 hours over 50 miles of ocean.

Whales have the greatest amount of sheer muscle power, but they are not the strongest animals for their size. The strongest animals for their size are insects.

Insects have been tested for their pulling ability on special insect-sized dynamometers. In these tests, the weakest insects can pull 5 times their own dead weight. A bee can pull 20.2 times its weight. And *Donacia*, a small leaf-eating beetle, can pull 42.7 times its weight. Since a horse can pull only 0.83 of its weight and a man 0.86, beetle-power is more than 50 times greater than horsepower or manpower.

Some insects have been tested for their lifting ability. Ants are easy to test because they normally use their jaws to lift and carry large objects. An ant can pick up a stone more than 50 times its own weight. It can carry that stone up a long tunnel and drop it outside its nest. If a human weightlifter had that much strength, he could lift a 5-ton elephant (with his teeth!) and carry it hundreds of yards up a steep hill.

Leaf-cutting ant at work: an ant can lift more than 50 times its own weight. *Ross E. Hutchins/Photo Researchers*

Beetles have been tested for their lifting ability by placing them in little harnesses with a weight attached. When tested this way, some beetles can lift 850 times their own weight! By comparison, a 200-pound man that strong could lift 82 tons on his back. An elephant could lift a navy destroyer.

The physical strength of insects makes other animals seem like hopeless weaklings. Where do insects get such phenomenal strength?

An insect's muscles are no stronger, gram for gram, than human muscles or the muscles of any animal. The difference lies in the way the muscles are attached. Our muscles, and the muscles of all animals with backbones, are attached to the bones inside our bodies. An insect's muscles are attached to the inside surface of its outer shell, or exoskeleton. This gives an insect's muscles greater leverage. As a result, its muscles work more efficiently than ours. Because of greater leverage, an insect's muscles can exert more power than equal weights of human, elephant, or whale muscle.

The strongest insect in the world is probably the Goliath beetle of Africa. There are no actual figures on this beetle's strength, but as the biggest insect, it probably boasts the most muscle power. It is said that if a door key is placed between a Goliath beetle's head and thorax, or back, when the beetle starts moving the key will bend.

There are many big tropical beetles similar to the Goliath beetle. All of them are extremely powerful for their size. In Africa, where farmers still use oxen as beasts of burden, children dig up these beetles from their burrows and make pets of them. They harness the beetles to toy wagons and carts and hold races in which the best beetle wins.

the animal that lives the longest

Very few animals live longer than humans. Among the mammals—animals that nurse their young—not one has a life span as long as ours.

This is surprising, since large animals tend to live longer than small animals of the same type. Humans are an exception. Quite a few mammals are bigger than humans, but their lives are shorter.

Even in ancient times before medical advances, people sometimes lived a century or more. No other mammal that we know of has ever approached the age of 100.

Apes have a life span about half as long as ours. Scientists estimate that a wild chimpanzee or gorilla may live 35 years. This is only a guess, since we have few accurate records for wild apes, or for most other wild creatures. Our knowledge of animal life spans comes mainly from captive animals in zoos and laboratories and from domestic pets.

In the wild, not many animals die of old age. Their lives are usually ended by enemies, accidents, or disease. A wild animal must be healthy enough to find the right kind of food or it will starve. In captivity, animals are fed regularly. If they are ill or injured, medical care can prolong their lives.

The oldest chimpanzee on record was a female who lived at the Yerkes Regional Primate Center in Atlanta until 1968, when she died at the age of 47. The oldest gorilla, a male named Massa, was still enjoying good health at the Philadelphia Zoo in 1981. Massa came to the zoo as a 5-year-old in 1935. He celebrated his fiftieth birthday in December 1980.

Massa, the oldest gorilla on record, celebrates his fiftieth birthday at the Philadelphia Zoo. *Philadelphia Zoo*

Two orangutans at the Philadelphia Zoo, Guas and his mate Guarina, lived well past 50. They came to the zoo in 1931, after spending several years at an ape station in Cuba. Guarina died in 1976, at the estimated age of 56. Guas died the following year, at the estimated age of 57. They were the oldest apes on record.

As a rule, small mammals lead short lives. One reason is that they tend to have small hearts, and small hearts pump faster than big ones. The smaller the animal, the faster its heartbeat. Its heart works harder, it breathes more often, and it burns up energy more quickly. In effect, the body of a small animal "wears out" faster than the body of a bigger animal. That's why an elephant lives 30 times longer than a mouse.

The mammals with the shortest lives are mice, rats, hamsters, guinea pigs, and shrews. In nature, they probably do not live more than a year or two at most. In captivity, they may live longer. A short-tailed shrew at the National Zoological Park in Washington, D.C., lived to the ripe old age of 3 years and 3 months. That's probably close to the maximum life span for a tiny shrew.

Some of the larger mice often live 3 years in captivity. Captive rats may reach the age of 4. And a small British rodent, the dormouse, has been known to live for 6 years.

Like humans, dogs and cats are exceptions to the rule that large animals live longer. Since cats are smaller than dogs and grow up faster, you would expect them to have shorter lives. But this does not seem to be the case. On the average, cats live longer than dogs. Many cats live well into their teens. Some live past 20. According to Dr. Alex Comfort, an authority on animal life spans, the oldest cat for which we have reliable records lived to the age of 31. However, some cat owners have claimed ages of 34 and even 36 for their pets.

Few dogs ever reach the age of 20. And oddly enough, small dogs usually live longer than big ones. The reason may be that larger dogs have relatively small hearts that must work extra hard.

The old rule of thumb that 1 year of a dog's life is equal to 7 years of a human's isn't strictly true, since some breeds live longer than others. Studies show that smaller breeds like spaniels and pekinese have an average life span of 11½ years. Larger breeds like mastiffs and wolfhounds average only 7 years. These are average ages, however, and a healthy dog will often live well into its teens. According to Dr. Comfort, the greatest age documented for a dog is 29 years.

Next to humans, the larger mammals are those that live the longest. Bears are believed to live between 30 and 35 years in the wild, if they survive illness and hunters. Domestic horses sometimes live past 40. A mule has been known to live 43 years, a donkey 47 years, and a Shetland pony 48 years. A horse that died in England in 1822 was said to be 62 years old, but experts believe that this was an exaggeration.

Rhinoceroses and hippopotamuses occasionally approach 50 years of age. The life span of the biggest whales is estimated at between 50 and 60 years, but it is hard to be sure, since there are no accurate records for whales.

The only mammal that comes close to the normal life span of a human is the elephant. Elephants grow up slowly—it takes about 25 years (some authorities say 30) for a young elephant to reach maturity. The average life span for a wild elephant is probably between 50 and 60 years, though some individuals live longer.

The oldest elephant for which there are reliable records was a female Indian elephant named Jessie. She lived at the Taronga Park Zoo in Sydney, Australia, for 57 years. Jessie's

LIFE SPANS OF MAMMALS

Mammal	Greatest Documented Age (Years)
Short-tailed Shrew	3
Dormouse	6
Opossum	7
Raccoon	14
Wolf	16+
Dog	29
Lion	30+
Cat	31
Brown Bear	34
Zebra	40
Racehorse	42
Mule	43
Fin Whale	43
Donkey	47
Chimpanzee	47
Shetland Pony	48
Rhinoceros	49
Hippopotamus	49
Gorilla	50
Orangutan	57
Elephant	77?
Human	114

age when she came to the zoo isn't known for certain. She was at least 12 years old and may have been 20. So she lived somewhere between 69 and 77 years. That's the greatest age ever recorded for any mammal other than a human.

The oldest human for whom we have reliable records was a Japanese man, Shigechiyo Izumi. He was born on June 29, 1865, and died on his birthday in 1979 at the age of 114.

Birds have a reputation for leading long lives, and often they do. Some birds live longer than most mammals. Here again, size is important. Bigger birds tend to live longer than smaller ones.

Small songbirds probably live an average of 2 to 3 years in the wild. In captivity they may live 10 to 15 years. The greatest age recorded for a songbird is 29, reached by an English chaffinch.

Parrots often live past 40. The oldest parrot whose age can be documented was a greater sulphur-crested cockatoo, a native of Australia. It lived for 56 years.

LIFE SPANS OF BIRDS

Bird	Greatest Documented Age (Years)
Hummingbird	8
Chaffinch	29
Domestic Pigeon	30
Emperor Penguin	34
Domestic Goose	35
California Condor	37
King Vulture	40
Herring Gull	41
Golden Eagle	46
Australian Crane	47
White Pelican	51
Vasa Parrot	54
Snake Eagle	55
Greater Sulphur-crested Cockatoo	56
Ostrich	62
Eagle Owl	68
Andean Condor	72+

Birds of prey also have long lives. An American golden eagle reached the age of 46; an African snake eagle lived to be 55; and a European eagle owl died at the proven age of 68.

The Methuselah of the bird world was a South American condor. This bird was already an adult when it took up residence at the Moscow Zoo in 1892. When it died in 1964, it was more than 72 years old.

Some bird owners have claimed even greater ages for their pets. There are reports of eagles, owls, vultures, and parrots living into their seventies and far beyond. Maybe they did.

A fish's age can be estimated by counting its scales, which grow year by year in a regular pattern. Minnows and other small fishes seldom live longer than a year or two. Fishes that grow longer than a foot usually have a life span of at least 4 or 5 years. There are reports of goldfish living 36 years in England and more than 40 years in China.

Big fishes may reach impressive ages. Carp have been known to live in ponds for 50 years or more. European river catfish, which weigh up to 400 pounds, have lived for more than 60 years.

The oldest fishes on record are giant sturgeons. Caviar is made from the female sturgeon's eggs. A beluga sturgeon, 14 feet long and weighing more than a ton, was determined by scale count to be about 75 years old. And a lake sturgeon caught in Wisconsin had an estimated age of 82 years.

To find animals that regularly live longer than humans, we must turn to the reptiles. The oldest creatures for which we have accurate records are turtles and tortoises. The common box turtle, found in woods and meadows in many parts of the United States, can live well past 100 if given the chance.

This box turtle, photographed at the Bronx Zoo in New York, was believed to be at least 110 years old. *New York Zoological Society*

Three box turtles have attained the proven ages of at least 118, 123, and 129.

The animal that lives the longest, as far as we know, is the giant land tortoise. The life history of one of these reptiles, an Aldabra tortoise, was carefully documented. It was called "Marion's tortoise" after the French explorer Marion de Fresne, who found the tortoise in 1766 when he visited the island of Aldabra in the Indian Ocean. Later, he presented the animal to the Port Louis army garrison on the island of Mauritius. In 1810, the tortoise was named as a national possession in the treaty by which the French granted Mauritius to England.

Marion's tortoise lived on Mauritius until 1918. It was accidentally killed at the age of more than 152 years—the greatest age definitely established for any animal.

Another giant tortoise that lived on the other side of the world, in the Galápagos Islands, was probably older. When it died, it was believed to be 176 years old.

OLDEST ANIMALS ON RECORD

Animal	Greatest Documented Age (Years)
Daudin's Tortoise	100+
Greek Tortoise	105
Box Turtle	118+
Box Turtle	123+
Box Turtle	129
Marion's Tortoise	152+
Galápagos Tortoise	176 (?)

champion survivors

Imagine the excitement if explorers discovered a living dino-saur in some far-off corner of the world. That's not likely. Scientists tell us that the last dinosaurs died out about 65 million years ago. All that's left are dinosaur fossils—bones and footprints preserved in stone.

The dinosaurs are gone, but other creatures from prehis-toric times still exist on earth today. They are called "living fossils," because they have survived so long with so little change. Living fossils look and act the way their ancestors did ages ago. They seem to be stranded in the dim and distant past.

About 200 years ago, explorers in New Zealand discovered a strange reptile unknown to the western world. It resembled a chunky big-headed lizard about 2 feet long. It had a crest of spines running from the top of its head to the tip of its tail.

The natives of New Zealand, the Maoris, knew this reptile well. They called it the *tuatara*, which means "bearing spines." And they said that tuataras live for centuries.

Scientists later found that the tuatara isn't a lizard at all. It is far more primitive than any lizard. The tuatara is a creature left over from prehistoric times. It belongs to an ancient group of "beak-headed" reptiles that once were common throughout the world.

Tuataras flourished 200 million years ago, when the first dinosaurs appeared on earth. In those days, there were thousands of different kinds of beak-headed reptiles, but they were already losing the struggle for survival. As "modern" reptiles such as snakes and lizards spread across the earth, the more primitive beak-headed reptiles could not compete for food or living space. Gradually they disappeared. Finally, only the tuataras were left, and they existed only in one place—the islands of New Zealand. There they had little competition from other animals and few enemies.

Enemies arrived during the 1800s, along with European settlers. The settlers brought with them animals such as dogs, cats, foxes, and weasels. None of these animals had existed in New Zealand before, and they began to prey on the native wildlife. Soon all the tuataras had vanished from the main islands of New Zealand.

Today they are found only on some small isolated islands off the New Zealand coast, where they enjoy strict govern-

Tuatara at the entrance to its underground burrow. These primitive reptiles have hardly changed since the days of the dinosaurs. *New Zealand Consulate General, New York*

ment protection. They live as their ancestors probably did, in dark underground burrows. They eat little—a few insects or worms a day. In warm weather, they spend hours sitting motionless among the rocks. During the winter they hibernate.

Tuataras have survived for more than 200 million years with only minor changes in their skeletons. They are the last of their kind—the most ancient reptiles living today.

Just before Christmas in 1938, a fishing boat pulled into the port of East London, South Africa, with one of the strangest catches of all time. Aboard was a peculiar fish that no one had ever seen before. It had bright blue scales, long fleshy fins, and a fanlike tuft at the tip of its tail. It was 5 feet long and weighed 127 pounds. It had been caught at a depth of 240 feet in the Indian Ocean, about 3 miles off the African coast.

The fish was taken to the East London Museum, where it was carefully examined. Experts were called in to examine it further. There was no question. It was a true coelacanth—a fish that was supposed to be extinct.

Coelacanths had flourished at the same time as the dinosaurs. They were thought to have died out with them. Now, for the first time, a living coelacanth had been hauled out of the sea.

Since then, dozens of these primitive fish have been caught in the Indian Ocean. They are believed to be the world's oldest living animals with backbones. Coelacanths first appeared in prehistoric seas about 400 million years ago. For the past 300 million years, these fish have hardly changed at all. By studying them, scientists have learned a great deal about the early development of animals with backbones.

Why was the coelacanth able to survive almost unchanged

for so long? Scientists aren't sure, but they can suggest some possible reasons. The coelacanth is able to adjust well to changes in the depth and temperature of the water. Its tough armorlike scales help protect it from enemies. Using its long fleshy fins as arms, it can creep along the sea floor to stalk food.

An interesting discovery about these fish is that they give birth to living young, as many sharks do. A coelacanth caught in 1975 was carrying 5 unborn babies, each about a foot long. Scientists now hope to raise coelacanths in captivity.

Few of us have ever seen a coelacanth or a tuatara. But many people have seen another living fossil—the horseshoe crab. Horseshoe crabs are common along eastern beaches from Maine to Mexico. They live in shallow water near shore, where they crawl along the bottom searching for scraps of food. Often they crawl up on the sand at low tide. Anyone can collect them by wading along the beach and picking them up.

These strange-looking creatures have been called "the crab that crawled out of the past." Scientists have found fossilized horseshoe crabs that crawled up on ancient beaches 425 million years ago. They were almost identical to horseshoe crabs living today. About the only difference between a modern horseshoe crab and its prehistoric ancestors is size— modern horseshoe crabs are bigger.

Horseshoe crabs are named for the horseshoe shape of their leathery shells. Despite the name, they are not true crabs. They are more closely related to land-dwelling spiders and scorpions.

The sea holds creatures even more ancient than the horseshoe crab. One is a common clam called *Nucula*. It is found

A horseshoe crab crawls ashore. It looks and acts like its ancestors from 400 million years ago. *New York Zoological Society*

nearly everywhere in the world, burrowing into the mud in shallow offshore waters. Fossil relatives of these clams have been discovered in ancient rocks dating back more than 450 million years. Judging from those fossils, nuculoid clams have changed little since that time.

The oldest living animal fossil ever discovered is another mollusk, *Neopilina galatheae,* which resembles a clam or oyster. This creature was thought to be extinct—until 1952, when scientists were dredging the ocean floor off the coast of Costa Rica. Along with the mud hauled up from a depth of 11,400 feet, they found a specimen of *Neopilina* alive and well.

Neopilina belongs to the most primitive group of mollusks known to science. Fossils from this group have been found in rocks dating back to the beginning of the Cambrian Period, about 570 million years ago, when the first complex living creatures appeared on earth. As far as we know, *Neopilina* is the only surviving member of that primitive group.

Today *Neopilina* exists only in the depths of the ocean,

where few other creatures live. Perhaps it has survived so long because it has little competition from other creatures and few enemies. In its safe refuge on the dark, silent ocean floor, it has become the world's champion survivor—a living creature that has remained almost unchanged for more than half a billion years.

LIVING FOSSILS

Animal	Earliest Known Appearance on Earth
Tuatara	200 million years ago
Coelacanth	400 million years ago
Horseshoe Crab	425 million years ago
Nucula	450 million years ago
Neopilina	570 million years ago

the biggest eaters

A bear will eat almost anything. It dines on fruits and berries in season, in addition to roots, seeds, grasses, vegetables, and nuts of all kinds, eating shells and all. It raids bees' nests for honey, catches salmon in streams, and searches for insects under stones and logs. The bear's menu includes delicacies such as ants, grasshoppers, crickets, mayflies, maggots, beetles, and grubs.

Bears are notorious for raiding garbage dumps and stealing food from campers. When they have a chance, they like to vary their diet with mice, squirrels, gophers, rabbits, and frogs. Occasionally bears will eat lambs, fawns, and young caribou.

Bears are classified as *omnivores*, which means they eat all kinds of plant and animal food. Rats and humans are also omnivores. The average adult American eats 1,445 pounds of food a year—815 pounds from crops and 630 pounds from animals. That's about 4 pounds of food a day for each adult.

Hunting animals such as dogs and cats are classified as *carnivores*, or meat-eaters. Lions eat meat almost exclusively. They feed on almost any prey that they can catch, including antelopes, gazelles, zebras, buffalo, wildebeest, baboons, hares, birds, and crocodiles. A male lion normally eats about 15 pounds of meat a day. A very hungry male may gorge himself with up to 90 pounds of meat—about one fourth his body weight—in one long, leisurely meal. After that, he can go for days without eating.

Grazing animals are called *herbivores,* or plant-eaters. They are strict vegetarians, and they usually eat quite a variety of plant food. A white-tailed deer is known to feed on at least 614 different kinds of plants.

A few animals have narrowly specialized diets. If they can't find exactly the right kind of food, they may starve. The koala of Australia eats nothing but the leaves of eucalyptus trees—not just any eucalyptus leaves, but only certain kinds. Since eucalyptus trees grow only in certain areas, most zoos can't keep koalas. In the United States, koalas have lived successfully only at the San Francisco and San Diego zoos, which are near large stands of eucalyptus trees.

The rare giant panda lives almost entirely on bamboo shoots. It seems that pandas can't do without this food, even in captivity. There are about 35 giant pandas living in zoos throughout the world, and bamboo is an essential part of their diet.

In the wild, giant pandas are found only in the remote mountains of southern China. Because of their peculiar eating habits, they are in danger of dying out. Chinese scientists reported in 1980 that at least a quarter of the world's population of giant pandas had perished because they could not find enough bamboo. Only a few hundred pandas still survive in the wild.

Another finicky eater is the vampire bat of tropical America. It dines on blood. Vampire bats usually attack horses, cattle, and barnyard poultry. They make a shallow wound

71

A koala eating a eucalyptus leaf. Each day an adult koala eats 2½ pounds of eucalyptus leaves—and that's all it eats. *Australian Information Service*

with their sharp teeth and lap up the blood with their tongues. Occasionally, a sleeping human will provide a meal for a vampire bat, without being aware of it. The wound is neither deep nor painful, but it can be dangerous because vampire bats sometimes transmit rabies. A vampire bat at the Bronx Zoo lived for 6 years on a diet of blood obtained from a local slaughterhouse. The blood was served each night in a shallow dish.

The amount of food that an animal eats depends on how big the animal is and on what kind of food it prefers. Large animals eat more than smaller ones. Plant-eaters need more food than meat-eaters, since meat provides a more concentrated source of energy. Animals in captivity need less food than wild animals, since they are less active.

The biggest eater among land animals is the elephant. An African elephant consumes between 300 and 600 pounds of plant food every day, depending on its size. In order to eat so much, the elephant's life becomes one long meal. Wild elephants spend about 16 hours a day browsing on leaves, shoots, bamboo, seeds, grasses, and fruit—almost any kind of plant food they can get.

An elephant gathers food with its trunk, which is sensitive enough to pluck ripe fruit from a tree. It drinks by sucking water into its trunk, which holds about a gallon and a half, and squirting the water down its throat. An elephant needs between 30 and 50 gallons of water every day.

Sharks have a reputation for being the greediest eaters. Most sharks will attack almost any kind of wounded and dying sea animal, including birds, porpoises, turtles, stingrays, and other sharks. Some sharks seem to gulp their food without paying much attention to what it is. Scientists at the American Museum of Natural History found the following food remains in the stomach of a tiger shark: fish bones, bird bones, feathers, grass, fragments of turtle shell, rusty tin cans, a dog's backbone, and the skull of a cow.

Killer whales are more ferocious than sharks. Most of the toothed whales live exclusively on fish, but killer whales seem to prefer warmblooded animals such as dolphins, porpoises, seals, sea lions, sea otters, and penguins. One killer whale caught in the Bering Sea had the remains of 32 adult seals in its stomach.

The world's biggest appetite belongs to the world's biggest animal—the blue whale. Blue whales have no teeth. They belong to the group called baleen whales, which includes fin whales, humpbacks, and gray whales. Instead of teeth, they have long strips of a substance called baleen hanging from the roofs of their mouths. These strips act as strainers. They make it possible for baleen whales to feed on tiny shrimplike creatures called krill.

During the arctic and antarctic summers, great masses of krill float near the surface of polar seas. As baleen whales swim along, they suck this krill into their gaping mouths along with sea water. The water then flows out of the whale's mouth through the baleen strainers, leaving the solid food behind.

No one knows exactly how much krill a blue whale consumes during the summer feeding months in the Antarctic. It probably gulps down at least a ton of krill every day. During the summer, blue whales put on gigantic amounts of weight. They eat constantly and may gain 30 to 40 tons. After a summer of serious eating, a blue whale may carry 20 tons of blubber. It lives off this blubber all winter, eating very little.

HOW MUCH MAMMALS EAT

Mammal	Average Body Weight	Average Daily Food Intake	Type of Food
Pigmy Shrew	2.5 grams	4.5–6.7 grams	Animal
Vampire Bat	28 grams	45–55 grams	Blood
Meadow Mouse	30 grams	19 grams	Vegetable
Dwarf Lemur	16 oz.	9 oz.	Mixed
Rabbit	72 oz.	18 oz.	Vegetable
Chimpanzee	100 lbs.	4.5 lbs.	Mixed
Virginia Deer	130 lbs.	9 lbs.	Vegetable
Lion	350 lbs.	15 lbs.	Animal
Bottlenosed Dolphin	350 lbs.	20 lbs.	Fish
Hippopotamus	4,000 lbs.	220 lbs.	Vegetable
African Elephant	8,000 lbs.	350 lbs.	Vegetable
Blue Whale	100 tons	1 ton	Krill

A ton of food a day is a world's record. And yet a blue whale may weigh 100 tons. It eats more than any other animal, but for its size it actually has a dainty appetite.

A blue whale eats about 1 percent of its body weight in food each day. An elephant eats about 4 percent of its body weight a day. In comparison, a mouse eats 25 to 50 percent of its body weight in food each day.

A small animal has a higher metabolism than a large animal—it burns energy faster. To replace its quickly depleted energy, it must eat plenty of high-energy food. Considering their weight, small animals consume more than big ones.

Shrews are the smallest mammals. They weigh between $\frac{1}{10}$ and $\frac{4}{5}$ ounce, depending on the species. For their size, they eat far more than any other mammal.

Shrews burn energy so fast, they will die of starvation if

kept without food for more than a few hours. To stay alive, a shrew may eat more than its own weight in food every day. The smallest shrews may eat almost twice their body weight in food each day. Their constant hunger drives them to attack animals much bigger than themselves. A short-tailed shrew will attack a mouse twice its size, paralyze the mouse with a poisonous bite, and devour it completely, bones and all. In captivity, shrews will eat each other.

Birds are popularly believed to be light eaters, but they also burn energy at a fast rate and need plenty of food. A bird's heart may beat faster than 400 times a minute, compared to about 70 beats a minute in a human. While a bird is flying, its heart may beat as fast as 1,000 times a minute.

To keep their bodies working at such a rapid pace, many birds consume more than half their body weight in food each day. A swallow may eat 1,000 mosquitoes a day, while a flicker will eat as many as 5,000 ants.

Hummingbirds, like shrews, consume more than their own weight in food each day. And they feed on nectar, the richest and most concentrated of all natural foods. If a 170-pound man burned energy as fast as a ruby-throated hummingbird, he would have to eat 285 pounds of hamburger every day.

Fast-growing baby birds need more food than adults. A pair of warblers will feed their growing nestlings a beakful of insects on an average of once every 4 minutes. Between dawn and dusk, the parents will bring more than 200 meals to the nest to satisfy their hungry young.

The biggest eaters of all for their size are newly hatched insect larvae. A honeybee hatches from its egg as a legless, wormlike larva. It starts life as little more than a living stomach, which must be fed constantly by a nurse bee that hovers overhead. As the growing larva lies in its wax cell, it is fed about 1,300 times a day. During its first 24 hours out of the egg, the tiny larva increases its body weight 5½ times. When it is 6 days old, it is 1,570 times bigger than when it hatched. By the end of the sixth day, it has spun a silk cocoon and has stored up enough energy to change into an adult worker bee.

A newly hatched caterpillar must feed itself. It is probably the world's hungriest creature as it nibbles away at leaves or other plant food. A caterpillar does almost nothing but eat until it is ready to spin its cocoon and change into a butterfly or moth.

The caterpillar of a Polyphemus moth consumes an amount of food equal to 86,000 times its birth weight during its first 24 days of life. If a human baby grew that fast and ate that much, it would need more than 300 tons of food by the time it was 3½ weeks old.

Moth caterpillar: the world's hungriest creature. *Karl H. Maslowski/Photo Researchers*

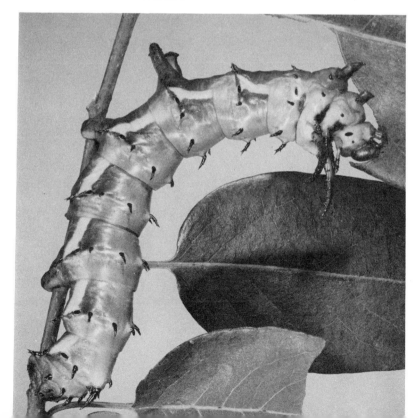

DINNER AT THE BRONX ZOO

The following diets are fed to each adult animal once a day. These diets vary according to size, sex, season, and activity of each animal. Captive animals eat less than wild ones.

Indian Elephant

150 pounds of hay
16 quarts of mixed ground grain
4–5 loaves of bread
3–4 heads of cabbage
pailful of raw potatoes, apples, and carrots

Gorilla

3 oranges
2 apples
2 carrots
1 stalk of celery
2 cans of prepared primate diet
¼ pound of prepared monkey chow
1 banana
1 cod-liver oil pill
few sunflower seeds
few peanuts
few grapes
1 egg (hard-boiled)
1 yam
a little cooked horsemeat

Sea Lion

10 pounds of mackerel
5 pounds of herring
2 vitamin capsules
salt tablets

Kodiak Bear

12 pounds of prepared bear chow
2 mackerel
2 chicken backs
2–3 pounds of grass
2 apples

Bald Eagle

5 days a week: 1 rat
1 day a week: horse spareribs
1 day grace

Python (8 feet long)

1 whole chicken or rabbit, 2½–4 pounds, once every 2 weeks

super moms

Most monkeys and apes give birth to just one baby at a time. One is about all they can handle, since they lavish care and attention on their young.

A chimpanzee is a doting mother. She will not let her baby beyond her reach until it is 5 or 6 months old. She nurses the young one until it is at least 4 years old. And she may carry it on her back until it is 5.

One or two babies at a time is the norm for many large mammals, including whales, dolphins, seals, bears, giraffes, camels, horses, elephants, and hippopotamuses. A lion usually has 2 or 3 cubs in a litter; a wolf has 4 to 6 pups. All of these animals look after their offspring for months or years. The young grow up slowly and have a fairly good chance to survive.

Of course, animals sometimes give birth to more than the usual number of young. As many as 7 lion cubs and 14 wolf pups have been reported in a single litter.

The biggest litter ever recorded for a domestic cat is 19 kittens, of which 15 survived. The record for a dog is 23 puppies, with 14 survivors.

The greatest number of young ever known to be born to a

wild mammal at a single birth were delivered by a common tenerec. These small insect-eating mammals are found only on the island of Madagascar. A tenerec usually has from 12 to 16 in a litter. One female is known to have given birth to 32 babies at one time.

As a rule, small mammals have the most babies. Shrews, mice, rats, and rabbits are all fast breeders, producing several large litters a year. These animals lead short, dangerous lives. They must produce large numbers of young to replace those killed by enemies, accidents, or disease.

A common meadow mouse, or vole, is able to have her first litter of young when she is scarcely a month old. She weans her babies when they are 2 weeks old. A week later she gives birth to a new litter. She can have as many as 17 litters in a single year, with 5 to 9 babies in each litter. At that rate, a meadow mouse could give birth to more than 150 babies in a year.

Another fast-breeding mammal is the golden hamster, a popular pet. Golden hamsters have an unusual family history. In 1930, a female and her 12 young were discovered in their nest near Aleppo, Syria. At the time, they were the only golden hamsters known to exist anywhere in the world.

The mother and young were taken to Hebrew University in Jerusalem for scientific study. Three members of the litter began to breed among themselves, and some of their offspring were sent to England in 1931. Some of their descendants, in turn, were brought to the United States in 1938. They were the first golden hamsters to arrive here.

Since then, no other golden hamsters have ever been found alive in the wild. Today, all the millions of golden hamsters in the world can trace their ancestry directly to that one mother hamster found in Syria a half century ago.

81

House mouse with newborn young. *Tom McHugh/Photo Researchers*

WILD MAMMALS AND THEIR YOUNG

Mammal	Average Gestation Period	Usual Number in Litter	Litters Per Year
Antelope	7–9 months	1–2	1
Bat, Little Brown	2 months	1	1
Bear, Black	7 months	2	1 every other year
Beaver	4 months	2–4	1
Chimpanzee	9 months	1	1 every 3 to 5 years
Deer, Whitetail	7 months	1–2	1
Elephant, African	20–21 months	1	1 every 4 years
Fox	54 days	3–8	1
Giraffe	15 months	1	1 every other year
Hippopotamus	8 months	1	1
Horse	11 months	1	1
Lion	3½ months	2–4	1
Mouse, House	21 days	4–8	5–8
Opossum	13 days	9–12	1–2
Rabbit, Cottontail	28 days	4–5	3–5

Mammal	Average Gestation Period	Usual Number in Litter	Litters Per Year
Rat, Brown	22 days	2–14	up to 12
Rhinoceros	18 months	1	1 every other year
Seal, Elephant	11 months	1	1
Seal, Harbor	9 months	1	1
Shrew, Common	19–21 days	3–10	2–3
Skunk, Striped	2 months	3–8	1
Squirrel, Red	36–40 days	3–6	2
Vole(Meadow Mouse)	21 days	5–9	up to 17
Whale, Gray	13 months	1	1 every other year
Wolf	2 months	4–6	1
Zebra	12 months	1	1

The number of young produced by a pair of birds at one time ranges from one to more than 20. An albatross lays just one egg a year. If anything happens to that egg, the albatross will not lay another egg until the following year.

Two eggs at a time are laid by most pigeons and doves, 3 eggs by gulls and terns, 4 to 6 eggs by familiar songbirds, and 8 to 12 eggs by many ducks and pheasants. The Hungarian partridge outlays them all, producing from 9 to 23 eggs in a single clutch.

Many birds raise two broods of young every year. A robin lays 4 eggs early in the summer. A few weeks later when her chicks are big enough to leave the nest, the robin lays another clutch of 4 eggs in the same nest.

Some birds are called "determinate" layers. They will lay only a certain number of eggs and no more. A crow, for example, lays 5 eggs and then stops. If one of the eggs is taken from the nest, the crow will not try to make up the loss.

WILD BIRDS AND THEIR YOUNG

Bird	Incubation Period	Number of Eggs Per Clutch	Number of Clutches Per Year
Albatross	77–80 days	1	1
Blackbird, European	15 days	4–5	2–3
Buzzard, Common	30 days	2–4	1
Cormorant, Great	28 days	3–4	1–2
Dove, Turtle	14 days	1–3	2
Duck, Common Eider	28 days	4–10	1
Duck, Mallard	26 days	7–14	1–2
Eagle, Golden	42 days	1–3	1
Falcon, Peregrine	29 days	3–4	1
Flamingo, Greater	32 days	2	1
Goldfinch, European	14 days	5–6	2–3
Goose, Greylag	28 days	3–7	1
Gull, Herring	26 days	2–4	1
Lark	12 days	3–4	2–3
Nightingale	14 days	4–5	1
Ostrich	45 days	12–15	1
Owl, Barn	32 days	4–6	1
Partridge, European	24 days	9–23	1
Pheasant, Ring-necked	25 days	8–15	1
Quail, European	20 days	7–12	1–2
Robin	14 days	4–6	2
Starling, European	13 days	6–7	1–2
Stork, White	30 days	3–5	1
Swallow, Barn	15 days	4–5	2–3
Swift, Common	20 days	2–4	1
Thrush, Song	14 days	4–5	2–3
Vulture, Griffon	51 days	1	1
Woodpecker, Green	18 days	5–7	1

Other birds are called "indeterminate" layers. If any of their eggs are taken, they will lay some more. Before they stop laying, they must have the proper number of eggs in their nest. A yellow-shafted flicker, for instance, usually lays 6 to 8 eggs. In an experiment, a flicker's eggs were removed from her nest as fast as she laid them, except for one "nest egg" that was always left in place. In her efforts to make up for the lost eggs, the flicker laid 71 eggs in 73 days.

Domestic fowl are also indeterminate layers that will keep on laying to make up for any egg losses. Humans learned long ago to take advantage of this trait, which is why hen's eggs are so cheap and plentiful. A hen keeps on laying because the farmer keeps on stealing her eggs. The best performance by a chicken is 361 eggs laid in one year. A duck did better than that, laying 363 eggs in a year. But the record is held by a specially bred quail in Japan that managed to lay 365 eggs in 365 days.

Birds and mammals have small families compared to most coldblooded animals. A sea turtle digs 3 or 4 nests during the breeding season and lays 100 eggs in each nest. A bullfrog lays as many as 20,000 eggs in a pond. A codfish pours from 4 to 6 million eggs into the sea at a single spawning.

These animals do not stay behind to guard their eggs or care for the newly hatched young. Only a few of the eggs and young survive, but that's enough to continue the species from one generation to the next.

The greatest egg producer among animals with backbones is probably the ocean sunfish. With its flat oval body, an ocean sunfish looks like a gigantic swimming pancake. It may easily be 10 feet long and weigh more than a ton. The biggest ocean sunfish ever caught weighed 4,400 pounds.

At a single spawning, an ocean sunfish lays as many as 300 million tiny eggs. The larvae that hatch from these eggs are about ¹⁄₁₀ inch long—barely big enough to see. A scientist once calculated that the size of a baby sunfish compared to its mother is like a small rowboat compared to 60 big ocean liners.

While most coldblooded animals lay eggs, there are quite a

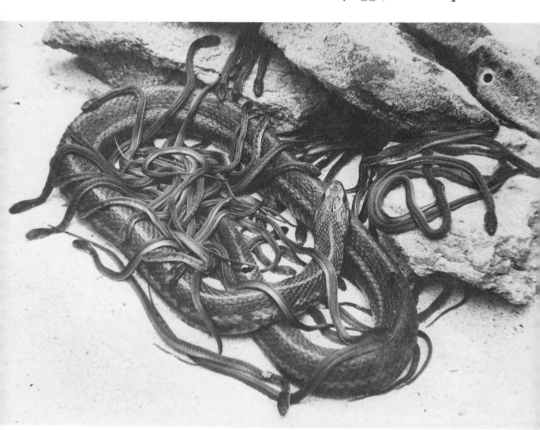

Common garter snake with newborn young: as many as 85 babies at a single birth. *New York Zoological Society*

SNAKES AND THEIR YOUNG

Snake	Usual Number of Young
Brown Snake	3–24 living young
Coachwhip, Eastern	8–24 eggs
Cobra, King	20–56 eggs
Copperhead	1–17 living young
Coral Snake, Eastern	3–12 eggs
Cottonmouth	1–15 living young
Garter Snake, Common	3–85 living young
Hognose Snake, Eastern	6–42 eggs
Kingsnake, Common	3–24 eggs
Mud Snake	15–104 eggs
Python, Rock	20–100 eggs
Racer	3–40 eggs
Rainbow Snake	22–50 eggs
Rat Snake	6–24 eggs
Rattlesnake, Timber	3–17 living young
Ribbon Snake	3–27 living young
Ringneck Snake, Eastern	1–10 eggs
Water Snake, Common	9–47 living young
Water Snake, Diamond-backed	18–62 living young

few fishes and snakes that give birth to living young. A 236-pound 19-foot-long anaconda at the Bronx Zoo once gave birth to 72 babies, each more than 3 feet long. Garter snakes sometimes have as many as 85 babies at a single birth. And a Florida green water snake once gave birth to 101 living young.

Live-bearing fishes include mollies, guppies, sharks, rays, and various kinds of rockfishes, such as the ocean perch.

Rockfishes produce more living young than any other animal. A female rockfish holds her developing eggs inside her body, and the babies hatch just before being born. When they leave their mother's body, they rise to the surface and live among the floating plankton, along with the newly hatched young of many other fishes. A large rockfish may give birth to more than 2 million babies at one time.

Most insects lay large numbers of eggs and never see their offspring. The social insects—ants, termites, and certain wasps and bees—are exceptions. Alone among the insects, they devote their lives to the care and protection of their young.

A beehive or ant nest is a teeming nursery, guarded by sentries. Inside, worker bees or ants scurry about as they look after developing eggs and feed the wormlike larvae that hatch from those eggs. Only one female in the nest, the queen, is capable of producing eggs. She may be the mother of every insect in the nest or hive.

During the summer breeding season, a queen honeybee may lay up to 2,000 eggs a day. If a queen bee lives for 3 years and lays eggs at a normal rate for 6 months a year, she will produce more than a million eggs in her lifetime. Unlike the eggs of an ocean sunfish, which are simply set adrift, the honeybee's eggs are carefully tended by worker bees. Each egg has a good chance to develop into an adult bee.

A queen bee has a small family compared to some termite queens. In a termite nest, the queen is hard to find, for she lies hidden deep within the nest. When the nest is established, the queen breaks off her wings and never leaves the nest again. She may lay only a few dozen eggs during the first year, giving birth to workers and soldiers who begin the task of enlarging the nest.

As the nest grows, so does the queen termite. With her huge abdomen swollen with eggs, she is by far the biggest termite in the nest.

The queens of some tropical termites are enormous. An old one may be 4 inches long and as thick around as a frankfurter. She is completely helpless, for her 6 spindly legs will not support her bloated body. Some termite queens are 160 times as big as their mates (the kings) and 2,400 times the size of worker termites. The nature writer Maurice Maeterlinck compared such a queen to "a whale surrounded by minnows."

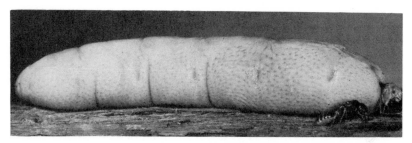

African termites: queen and king. The queen may lay more than 500 million eggs during her lifetime. *American Museum of Natural History*

In some species the queen lives with her tiny king in their royal chamber deep within the nest. They are surrounded by attendants that swarm about, feeding and grooming the queen and carrying off the eggs that flow from her body in a never-ending stream.

A termite queen may lay 10,000 eggs or more a day. The greatest number of eggs are produced by the queen of an

East African species called *Macrotermes bellicosus*. One of these queens can lay 43,000 eggs a day—an average of 1 egg every 2 seconds. And she may live as long as 40 or 50 years!

A tropical termite nest may have a population of millions of termites at any one time. And every termite in the nest may have the same mother—the fat termite queen. If the queen lives to a ripe old age, she can produce more than 500 million eggs, most of which hatch into worker termites.

That makes her the world's super mom.

the smartest animals

Almost any animal is smart enough to learn. A worm can learn—it's a slow learner, to be sure, but it *does* learn.

An earthworm's learning ability can be tested in a simple T-shaped maze. When a worm crawls up the T to the top, it can turn either left or right. If it turns left, it gets a mild shock. If it turns right, it finds a reward of food.

At first, an inexperienced worm will turn left about half the time and right half the time. Gradually, the worm will learn. It will turn right toward its food reward more and more often. Finally it will turn right almost every time.

The typical worm requires about 150 trials before it masters this lesson. Of course, some worms are smarter than others, and they learn faster.

Scientists have used mazes to test the learning ability of animals as different as ants, turtles, pigeons, rats, and monkeys. When an animal is tested in a maze, it is returned to the maze again and again until it learns which way to go. The faster the animal learns and the longer it remembers, the smarter it is.

Any animal from a worm on up can learn to master a T-shaped maze. Smarter animals can find their way through much more difficult mazes, with many turning points and blind alleys. When a rat is placed in a complicated maze, it investigates every single passageway and blind alley. It may spend 30 minutes exploring before it finds its food reward at the end of the maze. On its second trial, the rat may get through the maze in only 10 minutes. After a dozen trials, it will race through the maze in 30 seconds.

Mazes are one of many "IQ tests" used to measure animal intelligence. These tests can tell us a great deal about the learning ability and memory of animals. And yet animals are so different from each other, they can't always be compared by means of tests. A test that is fair to a dog may not be fair to a cat. It isn't easy to measure the intelligence even of our fellow humans. If you had to take a test designed for an Eskimo or an Australian Bushman, you might not do very well.

Another way to measure intelligence is to look at the size and structure of an animal's brain. An earthworm has only the primitive beginnings of a brain, but that's enough to learn a simple lesson. Among the higher animals—fishes, amphibians, reptiles, birds, and mammals—the brain becomes larger and more complex with each group. Reptiles have larger brains than frogs or fishes. Birds have larger brains than reptiles. And mammals have the largest and most complex brains of all. As a group, mammals are the smartest animals.

The largest brains on earth belong to the great whales. The heaviest brain on record, that of a 49-foot sperm whale, weighed 20.24 pounds. A 90-foot blue whale had a brain weighing 15.38 pounds. Next to the great whales, the elephant has the largest brain. An elephant's brain averages 11 pounds, but the biggest elephants have brains that weigh 13 pounds or more. A human brain, in comparison, weighs about 3.3 pounds.

Whales and elephants have larger brains than humans, yet they are not more intelligent. The overall size of an animal's brain is important, but the size of its brain compared to the size of its body is even more important.

Humans have the largest brains for their size. The brain of an average man is about $\frac{1}{50}$ of his total body weight. We might say that each ounce of brain is in charge of 50 ounces of body. In comparison, an elephant's brain is about $\frac{1}{1,000}$ the weight of its body. Each ounce of elephant brain must control 1,000 ounces of elephant body. So while an elephant's brain is larger than ours, the elephant doesn't have as many brain cells left over for intelligent behavior.

Even so, elephants are smart. In ancient times, the Greek philosopher Aristotle called elephants the smartest animals. Today, scientists still rank elephants near the top when it comes to rating animal intelligence.

Elephants are quick to learn, they can learn a lot, and they can remember for a long time. In India, work elephants used in forestry and road-building can remember the meanings of more than 200 commands. Experienced work elephants will often anticipate the wishes of their mahout, or trainer. They perform the right act even before they are given the command.

Elephants often show true understanding. As the writer Jack Denton Scott rode through the jungle on an elephant's back, his hat blew off. Without any orders from its mahout, the elephant stopped, picked up the hat with its trunk, and returned it to Scott.

Elephants are smart, but they don't have the brainpower of

the great apes. Chimpanzees, gorillas, and orangutans all have large, highly developed brains. In terms of intelligence and behavior, they seem closer to humans than any other animals.

At first glance, chimpanzees seem the cleverest of the apes. Wild chimps excel in the intelligent use of tools. They use carefully trimmed twigs to poke termites, a favorite delicacy, out of holes. They use long sturdy sticks to knock fruit down from trees. Chimps wipe dirt from their bodies and dab at wounds with handfuls of leaves. And they use sticks and stones as weapons to defend themselves.

Captive chimps are experts at imitating their human trainers. They can learn simple carpentry work, dress and undress themselves if given clothes, and do all kinds of tricks and stunts.

For years, scientists tried to teach chimpanzees to talk—not just to imitate words as a parrot does, but to speak and understand as a person does. These attempts failed. As the scientists found out, chimps lack the proper vocal cords. They can't say words because they can't make the right sounds.

Scientists finally took a different approach. In 1969, two psychologists at the University of Nevada announced that they had trained a female chimpanzee named Washoe to communicate. Instead of using spoken words, they communicated with Washoe by means of sign language, similar to that used by deaf people.

By using her own hands and watching her trainers use theirs, Washoe seemed able to understand words and use them herself. She even made up new words that she hadn't been taught. The first time Washoe saw a swan, she called it a

Washoe, the first "talking" chimpanzee, has a chat with her trainer, Dr. Roger Fouts. Washoe is using American Sign Language to ask Dr. Fouts for a "tickle." *Courtesy of Dr. Roger Fouts, Central Washington University, Ellensburg.*

"water bird." And she was able to carry on a simple conversation. Once when a plane flew overhead, Washoe looked up and then signed to her trainer, "You me ride in plane."

Washoe was the first "talking ape." Since then, scientists have trained a whole generation of chimpanzees, gorillas, and orangutans to communicate by sign language, by punching out words on computers, and by other means. Are these apes really learning to speak, as a child does? So far, scientists don't agree. Critics say that the apes learn individual words but do not learn to use language in a meaningful way.

Meanwhile, the experiments continue. A gorilla named

95

THE BRAINS OF MAMMALS

Adult Mammal	Average Brain Weight (in grams)
Mouse	0.4
Guinea Pig	4.8
Cat	31
Dog	65
Orangutan	340
Chimpanzee	380
Gorilla	540
Human	1,450
Dolphin	1,700
Elephant	6,000
Sperm Whale	9,200

Koko, trained in sign language at Stanford University, had a working vocabulary of 375 words by the time she was 7 years old. And she was leaning new words all the time.

Like Washoe, Koko coined her own words. When she tasted a stale sweet roll, she called it a "cookie rock." She also made comments and observations on the world around her. On a walk with her trainer, Koko stopped and then signed, "Listen—bird."

From time to time, Koko was given a standard intelligence test designed for preschool children who cannot yet read. She did as well as a human child a few months younger than she, scoring an IQ of between 75 and 85. Of course, some of the answers had to be changed to suit a gorilla. One question shows five pictures: ice cream, an apple, a block, a shoe, and a flower. The child (or gorilla) taking the test is asked to point out which ones can be eaten. Koko chose the apple and the flower. That's the right answer for her, since gorillas eat flowers.

Not long ago, chimpanzees were considered the smartest apes, followed by gorillas and then orangutans. But this ranking is no longer considered accurate. All three of the great apes are smart, and it's difficult to tell which is the most intelligent.

In recent IQ tests, chimpanzees, gorillas, and orangutans all achieved similar scores. On some tests, however, the orangutan outperformed the others. Psychologists at the Yerkes Primate Research Center in Atlanta found in one widely used test that on a rough scale of 100, orangutans scored 60, chimpanzees and gorillas scored 50, and gibbons scored 45.

Are apes the smartest animals? One animal, the dolphin, may be smarter. Next to humans, the dolphin has the largest brain for its size. Its brain is actually larger than a man's, but its body is also larger. A dolphin's brain is about $\frac{1}{85}$ the weight of its body. In comparison, a chimpanzee's brain is about $\frac{1}{150}$ its body weight, and a human's brain is about $\frac{1}{50}$ his body weight.

Everyone agrees that dolphins are extremely intelligent. But it is difficult to compare them to apes or humans since their way of life is so different. With their streamlined bodies, they are adapted to living in the sea. Even their brains are different. A dolphin's brain is wider than it is long—just the opposite of the brains of apes and humans. The part of a dolphin's brain that receives and analyzes sounds is larger and more complex than in most other animals. In the underwater world of the dolphin, sounds are extremely important.

Dolphins seem to learn faster than any other animal. On some tests, they learn almost as fast as humans. They seem to enjoy solving tough problems, and they become frustrated if they don't do well. One dolphin was being tested for his ability to recognize different visual patterns. When he made several errors, he apparently became angry. He grabbed a plastic pipe in his jaws and used it to smash the scientists' testing equipment.

Bottlenosed dolphins have become famous as the stars of seaquarium exhibitions, performing many complicated and spectacular routines. The dolphins catch on quickly, often imitating other dolphins without even being trained. Sometimes they invent their own games. A dolphin will tease a fish in its tank by dangling a piece of food as a lure, then snatching the food away. It will throw hoops and other objects out of the water for its human trainers to catch.

Dolphins exchange a wide variety of underwater sounds—whistles, clicks, blats, mews, yelps, wails, creaks, squeaks. Some scientists believe that the animals talk to each other, and that they may have a complicated speech pattern.

In recent experiments at the University of Hawaii, scientists have been training two female dolphins to communicate with humans by means of an artificial language. One dolphin named Phoenix is being taught sonic words that are generated in the water by a computer and sound like warbles, squeaks, and whistles. Each sound stands for a different

BRAIN WEIGHT COMPARED TO BODY WEIGHT

Adult Animal	Body Weight (in pounds)	Brain Weight (in pounds)	Brain Weight as a Percentage of Body Weight
Human	150	3.25	2.17%
Dolphin	300	3.75	1.25%
Chimpanzee	110	0.84	0.76%
Elephant	12,000	13.0	0.11%

Are dolphins the smartest animals? *Marineland of Florida*

word. Akeakamai (Hawaiian for "lover of wisdom"), the other dolphin, is learning the same words expressed by the arm signals of a trainer.

To start with, the dolphins learn the names of test objects such as balls, hoops, and frisbees. When the word for an object is given by sound or by an arm signal, the dophin has to touch the correct object with her nose. A special sound signal indicates yes for a correct response, or no for a wrong one. If the dolphin responds correctly, she gets a fish or a pat on the head as a reward. If she responds incorrectly and hears no, she may raise her head from the water and squeal in anger. She may even throw the object she is trying to name at the trainer's head.

After learning the names of objects, the dolphins learn to respond to simple commands such as, "Phoenix–ball–fetch–gate." This tells Phoenix to get the ball and carry it to a gate in the middle of the pool. Another command, "hoop–through," means to swim through the hoop. When Phoenix was given a new command, "person–through," a phrase she had never heard before, she swam over to one of the trainers and pushed him through the hoop.

The researchers in Hawaii believe that dolphins can understand the abstract meanings of words, since they respond correctly when words are used in new combinations. This suggests that the dolphins are learning to use language in much the same way as gorillas like Koko and chimpanzees like Washoe.

During these experiments, something unexpected has happened. Akeakamai, the dolphin trained to respond to arm signals, has also learned to recognize and repeat the computer sounds intended for Phoenix. When she sees a hoop, she makes the right sound for "hoop." If Akeakamai can learn to put these sounds together in a meaningful way, she may be able to carry on a two-way conversation with her human trainers.

If that happens, perhaps Akeakamai, the lover of wisdom, will be able to tell us a thing or two.

bibliography

Listed below are some of the works that were consulted in writing this book. The reader should note that figures on size, speed, strength, etc., may differ from one source to the next. Books preceded by an asterisk (*) are for younger readers.

BOOKS

Bourlière, François. *The Natural History of Mammals*, 3rd ed. (Knopf, N.Y., 1964)

Bridges, William. *The Bronx Zoo Book of Wild Animals*, (New York Zoological Society, N.Y., 1968)

———, *The New York Aquarium Book of the Water World* (New York Zoological Society, N.Y., 1970)

*Bunting, Eve. *The Sea World Book of Sharks* (Sea World, San Diego, Ca., 1979)

Burton, Maurice and Robert. *Inside the Animal World* (Quadrangle, N.Y., 1977)

Cahalane, Victor M. *Mammals of North America* (Macmillan, N.Y., 1961)

Carr, Archie. *The Reptiles* (Time-Life Books, N.Y., 1963)

Carrington, Richard. *The Mammals* (Time-Life Books, N.Y., 1963)

Comfort, Alex. *Ageing: The Biology of Senescence* (Holt, N.Y., 1964)

Douglas-Hamilton, Iain and Oria. *Among the Elephants* (Viking, N.Y., 1975)

Farb, Peter. *The Insects* (Time Inc., N.Y., 1962)

*Ford, Barbara. *Why Does a Turtle Live Longer Than a Dog? A Report on Animal Longevity* (Morrow, N.Y., 1980)

*Freedman, Russell, and James E. Morriss. *The Brains of Animals and Man* (Holiday House, N.Y., 1972)

*_____, *How Animals Learn* (Holiday House, N.Y., 1969)

Goodall, Jane. *In the Shadow of Man* (Houghton Mifflin, Boston, 1971)

Gordon, Bernard Ludwig. *The Secret Lives of Fishes* (Grosset & Dunlap, N.Y., 1977)

Guggisberg, C.A.W. *Wild Cats of the World* (Taplinger, N.Y., 1975)

Hahn, Emily. *Look Who's Talking!* (Crowell, N.Y., 1978)

*Hopf, Alice L. *Animal and Plant Life Spans* (Holiday House, N.Y., 1978)

*Hutchins, Ross E. *How Animals Survive* (Parents Magazine Press, N.Y. 1974)

_____, *Insects* (Prentice-Hall, Englewood Cliffs, N.J., 1966)

*Kevles, Bettyann. *Thinking Gorillas: Testing and Teaching the Greatest Ape* (Dutton, N.Y., 1980)

*_____, *Watching the Wild Apes* (Dutton, N.Y., 1976)

Lagler, Karl F., et al. *Ichthyology*, 2nd ed. (Wiley, N.Y., 1977)

Linden, Eugene. *Apes, Men and Language* (Saturday Review Press, N.Y., 1974)

McNulty, Faith. *The Great Whales* (Doubleday, Garden City, N.Y., 1975)

McWhirter, Norris. *Guinness Book of World Records* (Sterling, N.Y., 1979)

*Michel, Anna. *The Story of Nim: The Chimp Who Learned Language* (Knopf, N.Y., 1980)

103

Milne, Lorus J., and Margery Milne. *Patterns of Survival* (Prentice-Hall, Englewood Cliffs, N.J. 1969)

Ommanney, F.D. *The Fishes* (Time-Life Books, N.Y., 1970)

Orr, Robert T. *Animals in Migration* (Macmillan, N.Y. 1970)

*Patent, Dorothy Hinshaw. *Fish and How They Reproduce* (Holiday House, N.Y. 1976)

*_____, *Reptiles and How They Reproduce* (Holiday House, N.Y., 1977)

Peterson, Roger Tory. *The Birds* (Time Inc., N.Y. 1963)

Schaller, George B. *The Mountain Gorilla* (U. of Chicago Press, Chicago, 1963)

_____, *The Serengeti Lion* (U. of Chicago Press, Chicago, 1972)

Scheffer, Victor B. *The Year of the Whale* (Scribners, N.Y., 1969)

*Simon, Hilda. *The Racers: Speed in the Animal World* (Lothrop, N.Y., 1980)

*Smith, Howard E., Jr. *Giant Animals* (Doubleday, N.Y., 1977)

Welty, Joel Carl. *The Life of Birds* (Saunders, Philadelphia, 1975)

MAGAZINE ARTICLES

Benderly, Beryl L. "The Great Ape Debate," *Science 80*, July–Aug. 1980

Brower, Lincoln P. "Monarch Migration," *Natural History*, June–July 1977

Cauble, Christopher. "The Great Grizzly Grapple," *Natural History*, Aug.–Sept. 1977

Dawson, T.J. "Kangaroos," *Scientific American*, Aug. 1977

Eldredge, Niles. "Survivors from the Good Old, Old, Old Days," *Natural History*, Feb. 1975

Emlen, Stephen T. "The Stellar-Orientation System of a Migratory Bird," *Scientific American*, Aug. 1975

George, Jean Craighead. "Diners of Unlimited Diversity," *Natural History*, Jan. 1971

Gould, Stephen Jay. "Our Allotted Lifetimes," *Natural History*, Aug.-Sept. 1977

Keeton, William T. "The Mystery of Pigeon Homing," *Scientific American*, Dec. 1974

Kelsall, John P. "The Migration of the Barren-Ground Caribou," *Natural History*, Aug.-Sept. 1970

Kooyman, Gerald L. "Deep Divers of the Antarctic," *Natural History*, March 1976

———, "The Weddell Seal," *Scientific American*, Aug. 1969

Lindstedt, Stan L., and James H. Jones. "Desert Shrews," *Natural History*, Jan. 1980

Morgan, Stephanie. "The Sagacious Dolphin," *Natural History*, Aug.-Sept. 1968

Netboy, Anthony. "Round Trip with the Salmon," *Natural History*, June-July 1969

Premack, Ann James, and David Premack. "Teaching Language to an Ape," *Scientific American*, Oct. 1972

Schaller, George B. "This Gentle and Elegant Cat," *Natural History*, June-July 1970

Schmid, Rudolf, and Marvin J. Schmid. "Living Links with the Past," *Natural History*, March 1975

Willoughby, David P. "Animal Ages," *Natural History*, Dec. 1969

———, "Running and Jumping," *Natural History*, March 1974

Wursig, Bernd. "Dolphins," *Scientific American*, March 1979

index

(numerals in *italics* indicate photographs)

106

109

111

591
FRE

17613

Freedman, Russell

Animal superstars

591
FRE

Freedman, Russell

17613

Animal superstars

DATE	BORROWER'S NAME	
	Burks Kum	327
5/19/05	Jennifer	316

© THE BAKER & TAYLOR CO.